THE VISUAL CULTURE OF PAGAN

MYTHS, LEGENDS + RITUALS

# Pagans

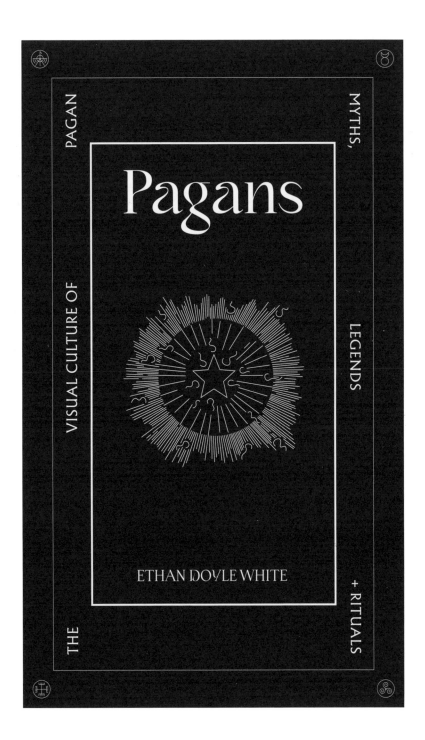

ETHAN DOYLE WHITE

# CONTENTS

# INTRODUCTION

AND HE RECEIVED THEM
AT THEIR HAND, AND
FASHIONED IT WITH A
GRAVING TOOL, AFTER HE
HAD MADE IT A MOLTEN
CALF: AND THEY SAID,
THESE BE THY GODS.

THE BIBLE (KING JAMES VERSION)

EXODUS 32:4

For followers of Abrahamic religions who
fear veering into idolatry, the material world
has long been a source of concern. In contrast,
there are, across the world, other religions -
those that Christians call 'pagan' - that have
wholeheartedly embraced the material universe
as something that can possess divinity, value
and meaning. These societies have sought
to build relationships with their divinities
through landscapes, sculptures and
performance, along the way creating many
of humanity's greatest artistic treasures.

**O**n an autumnal afternoon, a group of people parade through a city in the American Midwest. The banner they carry bears the declaration 'Pagan Pride', an affirmation of their identity as members of a growing religious minority. As well as their banner, their choice of clothes and jewelry highlights their difference from the country's Christian mainstream, displaying imagery and symbolism associated with ancient religions from the other side of the Atlantic.

Although these individuals use the term 'Pagan' to describe themselves, they represent a diverse range of religious identities. Some are Wiccans, members of a religion whose practitioners call themselves 'witches' and cast spells in their rites. Others are Druids, adherents of a nature-venerating tradition, who adopt the identity of the Iron Age ritual specialists of Western Europe. There are also Heathens, those who worship the old gods and goddesses once found among Germanic-speaking communities such as the Norse, while others venerate the Olympian divinities of ancient Greece. Also parading are members of the Goddess movement, dedicated to the worship of the feminine divine, and Neo-Shamans, whose focus is on visionary journeying experiences.

Modern Paganism comprises a family of related religions that have emerged during the 20th and 21st centuries, mostly in Europe but also in other parts of the world where European colonists settled in large numbers, especially North America. There is huge diversity among these modern Pagans, both in their practices and their beliefs, but there is also an underlying commonality. They all seek to resurrect something of the lost pre-Christian religions of Europe, North Africa and West Asia, adapting them for today's world. In doing so, they employ a range of sources, from historical texts and archaeological artefacts through to their own visionary experiences and to examples drawn from living polytheistic traditions. The use of the word 'Paganism' in this modern context is an act of reappropriation: taking a term with a long history of negative connotations and defiantly claiming it as a statement of self-definition.

⟨ *page 10*
Fresco, Villa of the
Mysteries, Pompeii, Italy,
*c.* 50 BC
*Many archaeologists believe that this fresco depicts a Bacchic rite devoted to the god Dionysus.*

**Virginia Lupu, modern Roma witches in Romania from the series** *Tin Tin Tin*, 2018–19

*Wearing white, these modern Roma* vrăjitoare *(witches) join together arrangements of white flowers and cast them into a stream. The choice of white indicates that their spell is designed as a blessing.*

**Three Roman Statuettes,**
*c.* **2nd century**
*These figures are less
than 20 cm (7 ⅞ in.) tall and
represent the deities Venus
(left), Mars (centre) and
Isis-Fortuna (right).*

\* \* \*

Historically, the term 'paganism' did not designate
a particular religion. Instead, it described a concept
with which Christians categorized those traditions
not worshipping the God of Abraham. In the early
centuries of the Common Era, this meant all the
world's religions except Christianity and Judaism:
the traditional belief systems of the Mesopotamians,
Egyptians, Romans and countless others. For the
early Christians, every deity other than their own was
a false god, typically a demon in disguise. In this, the
Christians were monotheists, believers in a single
divinity, whereas most other citizens of the Roman
Empire were polytheists, believing in multiple gods
and goddesses. This basic difference in outlook was
an important one, reflecting the radicalism of Judeo-
Christian thought.

The term 'pagan' became a weapon in Christianity's
rhetorical arsenal, part of a binary division through
which the early Christians perceived humanity. Those
wielding it thought they had a monopoly on theological
truth and believed in converting others – turning
polytheists into monotheists. For them, worshipping
deities other than their own was idolatry, clearly
forbidden in the Ten Commandments outlined
in Exodus, the second book of the Bible. After
Christianity became the Roman Empire's dominant
religion, the elasticity of the concept of paganism

**Offerings to Diana,**
**4th century**
*Hunters present offerings before the altar of the goddess Diana in this mosaic from the Villa Romana del Casale near Piazza Armerina, Sicily.*

became more apparent. In the 7th century, the rise of another monotheistic faith, Islam, led some Christians to regard it as something different from paganism, but others called Muslims pagan anyway. Even professing faith in Christ was not always enough to escape the accusation of paganism. During the 16th century, Protestants often declared that the Roman Catholic Church, with its intricate rituals, lavish images and veneration of the saints, was pagan.

Having emerged within the Roman Empire, much Christian terminology was shaped by Latin. The term 'pagan' is a good example of this. In Latin, a *paganus* was someone who lived in a *pagus*, or country district – in effect, a rustic. How this came to mean a follower of a religion other than Christianity or Judaism is not certain, but historians have made several suggestions. One argument is that the term *pagani*, understood as 'people of the place', gradually came to denote those who continued the religious traditions of their locality, whereas the *alieni* or 'people from elsewhere' were Christians, followers of an imported religion. Words

can shift their meaning over time, however, and by the 2nd and 3rd centuries, *paganus* had also come to mean 'civilian', a usage probably arising among the Roman military. Christians of the time thought of themselves as *miles Christi* (soldiers of Christ) and it is possible that they adopted *paganus* in reference to those who had remained civilians by failing to enrol in Jesus' army.

The term resurfaced among Christian writers in *c.* 370, by which point its earlier association with civilians may have been lost. Thus, many Christians assumed that the *pagani* were so-called because Christianity had caught on quickly in the cities, while the rural folk of the *pagus* lagged behind, continuing to worship their traditional deities. As Christianity spread, the term *paganus* also developed synonyms in other languages. In Greek-speaking areas, the terms *ethne* and *ethnikoi*, and later *Hellenes*, came to be used much like *paganus*. During the 4th century, Bishop Ulfilas (*c.* 311–*c.* 383), who was engaged in converting Germanic-speaking communities, translated *Hellenes* into Gothic as *haipno*, from which derives the Modern English term 'heathen'. Thus, wherever they went, Christians had the rhetorical tools for differentiating their community from the unbelievers.

Christianity rose to dominance in the Roman
Empire during the 4th century. Although previously
marginalized and persecuted, the Christian religion
gained respectability and status after Emperor
Constantine (*c.* 280–337), formerly a devotee of the
traditional Roman divinities, converted to it around
the 310s. Under one of his successors, Theodosius
(347–395), laws were introduced that prohibited various
non-Christian rituals. With elite patronage and laws
restricting its rivals, Christianity was able to flourish,
even as the Empire declined and ultimately collapsed
in the 5th century. Spreading beyond the Empire's
boundaries, the religion proved especially successful
in the northwest corner of the Old World: Europe,
North Africa and West Asia. Here, Christianity and its
Abrahamic siblings – Judaism and Islam – obliterated
and replaced virtually all earlier religions, from those
of Ireland in the west to Arabia in the east. In some
regions, the victory was so complete that historical
sources tell almost nothing of the pre-Abrahamic
traditions that once existed there – meaning that
what we do know is often only educated speculation
based on incomplete archaeological evidence.

Benvenuto Tisi da Garofalo,
*A Pagan Sacrifice*, 1526
*A libation of wine is poured over a severed goat's head, itself sitting on an altar, in this Renaissance painting of an imagined pre-Christian funeral.*

By the 15th century, pre-Christian religions had been almost entirely eradicated from Europe, surviving only among northern communities such as the Saami. It was in this context that Italian Renaissance humanists began taking a renewed interest in the mythologies of the ancient Greeks and Romans. Scenes borrowed from sources such as Ovid's (43 BC–AD 17) *Metamorphoses* or imitating ancient artefacts began appearing on a wide range of media, including furniture, sculpture, ceramics, paintings and prints. Some spaces, such as gardens and public fountains, were considered especially apt for the depiction of mythological scenes. There is no evidence that these artistic portrayals were accompanied by the worship of ancient Greco-Roman deities, and the depiction of biblical and historical scenes remained highly popular. However, the growing artistic interest in the Classical world played an important role in shaping Europe's changing attitudes to its past.

Across Europe, Greco-Roman mythology reached the height of its artistic popularity in the 17th and 18th centuries, used by socio-economic elites to demonstrate their education, refinement and taste. Soon, interest in the pre-Christian religions of other regions was also stimulated. The translation of medieval Icelandic manuscripts from the 17th century onward introduced many Europeans to the gods and goddesses of the pre-Christian Norse, and by the 18th century these deities were also appearing in new paintings and sculptures – often anachronistically clothed in Classical dress. The early 19th-century Romantic movement encouraged interest in the pre-Christian religions of linguistically Slavic and Celtic societies, too, about which little was reliably known. Tied in with burgeoning cultural nationalisms and nostalgia for the distant past, this newfound appreciation of pre-Christian societies helped fuel the emergence of modern Paganism in the 20th century.

★ ★ ★

Rising interest in Europe's own pre-Christian traditions was accompanied by growing awareness

of non-Abrahamic religions elsewhere in the world.
As Europeans spread into the Americas, Asia, Africa
and Australasia – first as explorers and later as
conquerors and colonists – they were once again
confronted with societies that were not Christian,
Jewish or Muslim, societies that these Europeans
typically labelled 'pagan'. In India, for example,
European Christians encountered a panoply of gods
and goddesses – part of what is now called Hinduism,
but often referred to by 19th-century British writers
as 'Hindoo paganism'.

In each of these continents, Christian missionaries
soon set out to convert the nonbelievers. Although
they established Christianity as the world's first truly
global religion, the missionaries did not prove as
successful as their late antique and medieval forebears
in eradicating existing non-Abrahamic traditions.
While there are, for example, thriving Christian and
Muslim communities in India, Hinduism remains the
country's dominant belief system – and the world's
largest non-Abrahamic religion. In Nigeria, a host of

< ***Krishna Stealing the Milkmaids' Clothing,*** **18th century**
*A Mughal-style Indian artwork depicts Krishna, an avatar or earthly incarnation of the god Vishnu.*

> **Utagawa Hiroshige,** ***Oji Inari Shrine*, 1857**
*This woodcut of a Shinto shrine devoted to the* kami *spirit Inari is from Hiroshige's series* One Hundred Famous Views of Edo.

African traditional religions persevere amid Abrahamic dominance, with many Nigerians combining Christianity and Islam with the traditional religious practices of their ancestors. In Japan, meanwhile, Christianity and Islam have struggled to establish anything more than a minor foothold. Shinto, the country's traditional polytheistic system, remains its largest religion – albeit often operating in a syncretistic and complementary relationship with Buddhism.

By the latter half of the 20th century, Europeans and other Westerners were increasingly hesitant to describe religions such as Hinduism, Shinto or Vodou as pagan. There was an acknowledgment that the term bore negative and Eurocentric connotations, and that it was inappropriate for a world of postcolonial states and interfaith dialogue. Academic disciplines such as the study of religion were shedding much of the Christian terminology they had inherited, while the growth of modern Pagan movements in Europe and North America had invested the term 'paganism' with new meanings.

This is not to say that 'paganism' has been completely retired from the Christian lexicon. There are still practitioners, especially Protestant Evangelicals but also Roman Catholics and Orthodox Christians, who use the term 'pagan' in ways familiar from Christian history. Ironically, this broad-brush application of the word is also embraced by some modern Pagans, who are keen to highlight common ground between themselves, the extinct pre-Christian systems of the Old World and living non-Abrahamic traditions such as Shinto, Santería or the traditional religions of the Navajo, Yoruba and Māori. Members of these living systems have sometimes cooperated with modern Pagan groups – some Hindus and European Pagans have, for example, collaborated to oppose Christian proselytization in India – although so far non-Abrahamic traditional religionists have made no widespread attempt to follow modern Pagans in reappropriating the term 'pagan' itself.

* * *

Paganism is a deeply problematic concept. It forces people into a Christian missionary mindset, one that divides Christian from non-Christian, true religion from superstitious idolatry. Unsurprisingly, anthropologists and scholars of religion no longer employ it as a cross-cultural category, preferring to talk of African traditional religions, East Asian religions or Indigenous American religions, for example. Where the word lingers is among historians and archaeologists discussing European religions encountered by Christianity in antiquity and the Middle Ages – although even here, other terms such as 'traditional religion' are increasingly popular replacements. Safer terminological territory is only reached when talking of 'modern Paganism', with the standard scholarly convention now being to refer to these new religious movements in capitalized form as 'Pagan' and to the general Christian concept in lower case form as 'pagan'. This helps to clarify that the former is an identity that people usually claim for themselves; the latter is one that is imposed on them from the outside.

**Kathari Deftera
in Nedousa**

*Locals at Nedousa, Greece, celebrate Kathari Deftera (Clean Monday) each February
or March. Celebrations at Nedousa involve a symbolic performance of the wedding
of Demeter and Jason, the consummation of which is pictured here.*

**Rodnover Kupala
Celebration**

*Russian followers of Rodnovery, a modern Pagan religion inspired by the pre-Christian traditions of linguistically Slavic societies, celebrate their midsummer festival, Kupala, at a forest near Bronnitsy, Moscow Oblast.*

One thing that unites these diverse phenomena, whether extinct pre-Christian traditions, modern Pagan religions or living non-Abrahamic traditional systems, is their typical embrace of the material world. All make use of objects, buildings and environments to maintain relationships between humanity and 'other-than-human persons', whether they be gods, ancestors or spirits, or even animals, plants and rocks. These traditions are largely polytheistic and repeatedly portray supernatural figures in visual form, from the marble sculptures of the Classical world to the intricate timber carvings of the Māori meetinghouse. Many of these religions recognize the presence of divinity within the natural environment, treating particular areas as sacred sites, whether that be Japan's Mount Fuji or a wooded grove in Russia's Mari El Republic. They often use rituals to engage with divine beings or seek knowledge from the deities through divination, including, for example, the West African *Ifá* system or the yarrow stick cleromancy of the Chinese *Yijing*.

Many of these traditions fear supernatural malevolence in the form of the witch – although in the unusual case of Wicca, the identity of the witch is actively embraced. Practitioners of these religions often gather communally to celebrate festivals: great public processions akin to those that once graced ancient Greek and Mesopotamian cities can still be found in the urban hubs of India and Japan today. Members of these traditions will adapt their physical appearance to display their allegiance to the community or their specific role within it, exemplified by the headdresses worn by various Siberian ritual specialists or the hammer of the god Thor worn by modern Heathens. Many of these religions also teach that there are other realms to which humans can travel – even if only after death, as in the case of the ancient Egyptian afterlife. While there are vast cultural, linguistic and aesthetic differences between the many religious communities whom Christians have labelled 'pagan', there is also a raft of recurring features, which, when considered alongside each other, offer deeper insight into the complexities of the human experience.

PART ONE

# ANCIENT WAYS

1
GODDESSES + GODS

2
MYTHS + LEGENDS

3
NUMINOUS NATURE

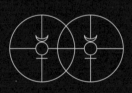

/ˈeɪnʃ(ə)nt/adjective

*Inherited from the distant past.*

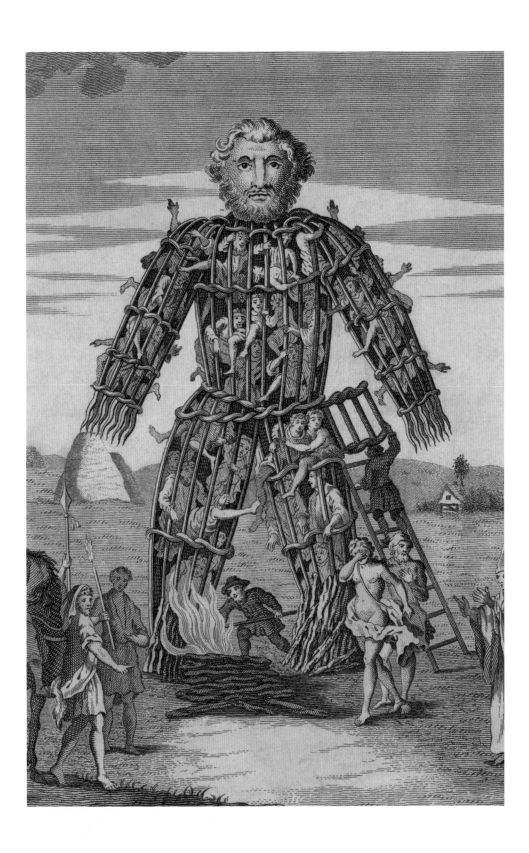

# GODDESSES + GODS

I AM SHE THAT IS THE
NATURAL MOTHER OF
ALL THINGS, MISTRESS
AND GOVERNESS OF ALL
THE ELEMENTS, THE INITIAL
PROGENY OF WORLDS,
CHIEF OF POWERS DIVINE,
QUEEN OF HEAVEN!

*LUCIUS APULEIUS, METAMORPHOSES, OR THE GOLDEN ASS*

BOOK I I, CHAPTER 47, TRANS. WILLIAM ADLINGTON

In contrast to Christian monotheism, polytheistic religions embrace a cosmos full of divine beings, among them both female goddesses and male gods. This panoply of deities reflects the complexities of the natural world and of human society, with different divinities often associated with specific forces of nature, professions or facets of life. In seeking the aid of these powerful entities, worshippers have repeatedly portrayed them in a diverse range of artistic styles and mediums.

**E**ntering the Parthenon atop the Acropolis of Athens, Greece, an ancient visitor would have passed into the inner chamber and beheld the huge statue of the goddess Athena, patroness of the city and a deity of wisdom and warfare. Today, a pilgrim to one of the many temples of Kolkata, India, will proceed to the inner sanctum, carrying offerings to present before the statue of Durga, a maternal figure who, like Athena, is a goddess of war. For many Christians, the worship of these goddesses constitutes pagan idolatry, but for those involved in such traditions they are vibrant and vital aspects of a well-rounded spiritual life.

\* \* \*

Many polytheistic religions allow for the existence of a vast number of divinities. From ancient Mesopotamia, for example, the names of more than two thousand have survived. The sheer number of deities often present in such religions makes it impractical for anyone to venerate them all equally. Instead, practitioners will typically devote their attentions to just one or a small number of these gods and goddesses.

Often a deity will be chosen because of its links to a specific profession. Among the Yoruba people of West Africa, for example, the god Ogun is regularly worshipped by blacksmiths due to his association with iron. Alternatively, a deity may be chosen because it is highly popular or even a patron figure in a particular place, such as Athena at Athens. A worshipper may also turn to a deity who specializes in certain tasks, whether that be offering protection during childbirth, healing the sick or helping someone pass an exam. Sometimes worshippers strike bargains with a deity, agreeing to provide them with offerings in turn for a service rendered. Ultimately, gods and goddesses are commonly seen as powerful allies in coping with the trials and tribulations of everyday life.

Many deities are associated with a specific location, sometimes being worshipped there and nowhere else. Other divinities are popular far and wide, their worship spread by migrants, traders or invaders. Initially, the maternal goddess Isis was venerated in Egypt, for

< *page 27*
*The Wicker Colossus of the Druids*, 18th century
This engraving is one of several to illustrate a volume of Thomas Pennant's A Tour in Wales, 1781.

< *page 28*
William-Adolphe Bouguereau, *The Birth of Venus*, 1879
A dolphin pulls the newly born goddess Venus through the sea towards Paphos.

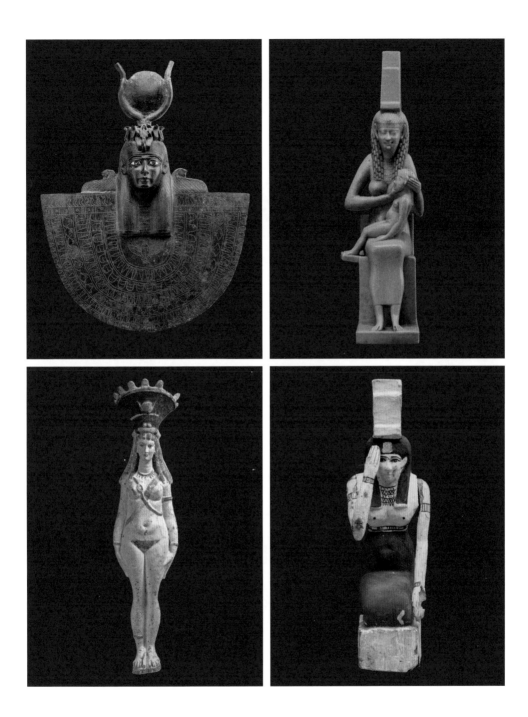

**Four Sculptures
of the Goddess Isis**

*Isis was known as Aset, or 'Queen of the Throne', to the ancient Egyptians. Growing
in popularity over time, she was depicted in various ways. Here, clockwise from top
left, she is represented wearing a headdress in an aegis from c. 924-600 BC, suckling
her son Horus and kneeling in mourning in two Ptolemaic sculptures and taking the
syncretic form of Isis-Aphrodite in a terracotta figure from the Greco-Roman period.*

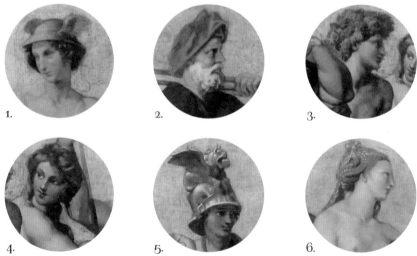

1.

2.

3.

4.

5.

6.

## DECODING
THE OLYMPIAN
GODS +
GODDESSES

Painted on the ceiling of the Villa Farnesina in Rome in 1517–18, the *Council of the Gods* is a fresco by the school of Raphael. It depicts the gods of Mount Olympus after Zeus has accepted the mortal Psyche (pictured on the far left), and Hermes gives her the drink of immortality.

7.

8.

9.

10.

11.

12.

1. Hermes / Mercury
2. Hephaestus / Vulcan
3. Dionysus / Bacchus
4. Apollo
5. Ares / Mars
6. Aphrodite / Venus

7. Hades / Pluto
8. Poseidon / Neptune
9. Zeus / Jupiter
10. Artemis / Diana
11. Hera / Juno
12. Athena / Minerva

**The Jade Emperor**
*Three images of the divine ruler of heaven and earth, also known as Yuhuang Dadi, in Chinese polytheistic traditions.*

example, but her worship ultimately spread throughout the Roman Empire, reaching as far north as Britain. Originally associated with royalty, she later came to be more widely invoked for healing and protection. Deities can also be linked to forces of nature or celestial bodies, especially the sun and the moon. Solar divinities are quite common and sometimes became preeminent in their respective pantheons: in the 14th century BC, for example, the Egyptian king Akhenaten (1372–1336 BC) insisted that the sun god Aten be worshipped, largely at the expense of other deities. Although the sun is often associated with male divinities, in Japanese Shinto the sun is personified by a goddess, Amaterasu, who plays a central role in important mythological stories.

In an attempt to understand the complex plethora of deities, people have categorized them into pantheons, often linked through family relationships. Thus, in ancient Greece, a mythological framework emerged in which Zeus was the king of the Olympian divinities, the goddess Hera was his wife, and the gods Ares and Hephaestus were his children. Other pantheons reflected the bureaucratic relationships evident in the societies that compiled them. In Chinese polytheistic

**Great Dish, AD 4th century**
*One of thirty-four large pieces of Roman silver tableware discovered in Mildenhall, England, this elaborately carved dish measures 60.5 cm (24 in.) in diameter. The head of Oceanus, god of the ocean, is carved in the centre, surrounded by sea nymphs and tritons.*

**Pediment of the Temple of Sulis Minerva, Bath, England, c. AD 1st century**
*This temple pediment, featuring a carved head, often identified as a Gorgon, was originally part of the Roman temple of Sulis Minerva in Bath, England.*

religions, for example, the Jade Emperor is often regarded as the chief deity tasked with governing heaven and earth and is assisted in this complex task by a range of officials and ministers.

Another way in which polytheistic societies have sought to understand this theological complexity is by equating their own deities with those of other linguistic or ethnic groups. In ancient Mesopotamia, for example, certain divinities came to bear both Sumerian and Akkadian names, possibly reflecting the merger of deities who were previously separate. Thus, the Sumerian goddess Inanna merged into the Akkadian goddess Ishtar, both having associations with beauty, love and sex. Similarly, as the Roman Empire spread, the Romans engaged in what came to be called *interpretatio Romana*, identifying the deities they encountered with those with whom they were already familiar. In Britain, for example, the Romans identified the local water goddess Sulis with their own deity Minerva. Curse tablets found at the thermal springs of Aquae Sulis in modern-day Bath, England, reveal that Romano-Britons approached Sulis Minerva in the hope of punishing those who had wronged them.

When dismissing these religions as pagan idolatry, Christian observers often failed to appreciate the

*Gods to be Worshipped in the Evening*, 1880s
The three key Hindu deities - Brahma, Vishnu and Shiva - are each depicted seated on a vahana or animal vehicle.

complexities and variation within polytheistic cosmologies. While polytheists often believe that the gods and goddesses each represent distinct, independent individuals, they sometimes adopt an approach termed 'henotheism', maintaining that one of the deities, especially a creator divinity, is preeminent among them. This is the stance found in many West African traditional religions and those African diasporic traditions descended from them. Examples include Haitian Vodou, in which the multitude of *lwa* deities are ranked below a single creator god, Bondye. Elsewhere, polytheists have argued that there is an inner unity behind the many deities. In the 3rd century, for example, Neoplatonist philosophers around the Mediterranean area were arguing that, even though many gods and goddesses existed, there was a single divine force underlying all things. Similarly, in modern Hinduism a common belief is that all the divinities are manifestations of a single supreme divine reality, Brahman.

**Pacific Northwest Ravens**
*These 19th-century rattles were probably used in longhouse dances. One is Tsimshian (left), one Haida (right) and the third potentially either Tsimshian or Haida (centre).*

Polytheistic societies have taken different approaches to portraying deities. Some depict them in an aniconic way, using natural features such as rocks, trees or a flame to represent a divinity. Others perceive them anthropomorphically, taking human form. The ancient Greeks and Romans, for example, portrayed their gods and goddesses in highly naturalistic sculptures, depicting them as idealized humans. Sometimes, deities are clearly humanoid but with unusual additions. This is very evident in Hinduism, where the god Vishnu has blue skin and the god Brahma possesses four heads. In these instances, extraordinary features help distinguish the divinities from humanity.

In a few cases, polytheistic religions have portrayed their deities in a theriomorphic or zoomorphic fashion, modelling them on other animal species. This approach was common in ancient Egypt, where divinities were often depicted in animal form, especially in votive sculpture. Cat figurines were, for example, commonly used to signify the goddess Bast. At other times, deities were portrayed as a mix of human bodies and animal heads, among them the falcon-headed Horus and the jackal-headed Anubis. Zoomorphic figures also appear in the religions of other parts of the world. The Raven, for example, is a recurring character among indigenous mythologies from the Pacific Northwest, perceived as having played a formative role in creating the world.

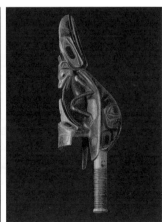

## PROFILE
EGYPTIAN GODS
+ GODDESSES

More than a thousand deities are recorded from ancient Egypt, where their role was to uphold *maat*, the cosmic order. Egyptologists argue that many of these divinities arose as the patrons of particular locations before Egypt's political unification saw them combined into an interconnected pantheon. Various deities also syncretized with others, exemplified by the blending of Ra and Horus to form Ra-Horakhty, a god depicted on this stele from the Third Intermediate Period.

**ISIS**
This wooden figurine (666–
630 BC) depicts Isis with Horus.
Isis was initially a minor goddess
but grew into one of the major
figures of the Egyptian pantheon.

**OSIRIS**
This figure of Osiris, a god
associated with fertility, dates
from 522–343 BC. The story of
Osiris's death and resurrection
is an influential Egyptian myth.

**HORUS**
Sometimes presented as the son
of Osiris and Isis, the god Horus
is associated with kingship and
the sky. His falcon head is shown
clearly in this Ptolemaic amulet.

**SET**
This statue (1279–13 BC) features
Set, a god of warfare, storms and
the desert. Set's murder of his
brother Osiris may have added
to his growing unpopularity.

**ANUBIS**
Depicted here in a figurine of
664–630 BC, the canine-headed
god of the dead Anubis is the
creator of embalming and leads
the dead into the afterlife.

**SEKHMET**
Bearing the head of a lioness,
as can be seen in this figure of
664–630 BC, Sekhmet is a fierce
goddess associated with healing,
disease and warfare.

◁ **Greek Calyx-Krater,**
  *c.* **4th century** BC
  *This terracotta vessel was*
  *used for mixing wine and water*
  *and depicts the hero Heracles'*
  *death and apotheosis, or*
  *elevation to divine status,*
  *on Mount Olympus.*

▷ **Roman Head of Emperor**
  **Augustus,** *c.* **27** BC–AD **14**
  *This small head is likely of*
  *Augustus, the first of the*
  *Roman emperors, who*
  *was posthumously deified.*

Boundaries between humanity and the deities are not always clear-cut, with myths telling of humans born to partially divine ancestry. One of the well-known heroes of ancient Greek mythology, Heracles, was the son of the god Zeus and the mortal woman Alcmene. In other cases, certain humans – especially members of powerful elites – were themselves deemed divine. In ancient Egypt, the kings were worshipped as beings set apart from normal humanity, while for the first two centuries of the Roman Empire, most emperors were declared gods after they died. In some cases, figures other than leaders were deified on their deaths. In the 2nd century, for example, Roman Emperor Hadrian (76–138) declared that a young man whom he loved, Antinous, had become a god after drowning in the River Nile. These deified humans can continue to attract worship long after their deaths. The Chinese general Guan Yu (160–220) died in the early 3rd century, but is still widely worshipped across the Chinese world as Guandi, a god of war, literature and commerce.

★ ★ ★

Many polytheistic traditions maintain that images of their deities are not lifeless portrayals but are

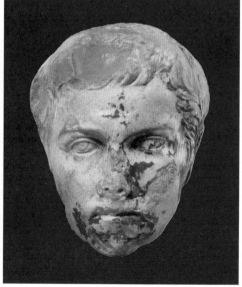

**Hindu *Murtis***
*In Hinduism, deities are believed to inhabit their statues, which are called* murtis. *Two of these (left and right) depict the elephant-headed god Ganesh; the third (centre) is Gauranga, a devotee of the god Krishna.*

inhabited literally by the divine being itself. This idea was apparently present in ancient Mesopotamia, where one poem recounts how Erra, a god of pestilence, convinced the god Marduk to 'leave' the image in which he dwelt. In today's world, this approach is evident in Hinduism, where statues of deities (known as *murtis*) are typically believed to contain the presence of the god or goddess. When a *murti* is being created, specific ritual instructions are followed to ensure that it is fit to house the deity, with the final act involving a priest 'opening' the eyes of the *murti* so that it may see. For many Hindus, the *murti*'s ability to see and be seen is especially important, allowing devotees to receive the blessings of the indwelling divinity.

In regions where Abrahamic religions wholly replaced their polytheistic predecessors, images of the deities often underwent a desacralization and came to be viewed in a different light. The rise of Renaissance humanism in 15th-century Italy encouraged greater interest in the artworks of Classical antiquity, including many that depicted gods and goddesses. Renaissance collectors not only gathered ancient sculptures but also commissioned the artists of the day, including well-known names such as Sandro Botticelli (1445–1510) and Michelangelo (1475–1564), to create new images of these deities. Unlike their ancient predecessors, these

# DECODING
## HINDU GODS + GODDESSES

The Hindu pantheon is incredibly diverse, home to a vast selection of deities. Some divinities – such as the sky god Indra – were of key importance in the Vedas, ancient texts that underlie much of Hinduism but have since declined in popularity. Other gods and goddesses are localized, receiving little devotion outside a particular area. In modern Hinduism, the most widely worshipped deity is Vishnu, a god who comes to Earth in the form of avatars such as Rama and Krishna, often to do battle with demonic forces threatening humanity. The second most popular is probably Shiva, a god of destruction who, like Vishnu, is associated with slaying dangerous beings. Devotees of Vishnu are typically called Vaishnavites, while Shiva's counterparts are known as Shaivites. Hindu theology typically holds that all these varied deities are personifications of a single divine reality, often called Brahman. Thus, Hinduism has largely tolerated the worship of many divinities in a way not possible within most Abrahamic religions.

*BRAHMA*
The creator god Brahma forms the *trimurti* with Vishnu and Shiva. His four mouths, which created the four Vedas, are shown in this painting from a *ragamala* (c. 1675).

*VISHNU*
This 1886 print depicts Vishnu, a preserver god known for incarnating on Earth as an avatar when the world's cosmic order is under threat.

*SHIVA*
A god of destruction, Shiva is described as living on Mount Kailash in the Himalayas as a Yogi. This painting of Shiva dates from *c.* 1760.

### LAKSHMI
Lakshmi, pictured here in a print of *c.* 1880, is the goddess of good fortune and wealth. She is the wife of Vishnu and is said to take different forms to be with him.

### KALI
The frightening goddess Kali is associated with death and destruction as well as motherly love. This print of *c.* 1879 shows her typical blue-black skin.

### GANESHA
Often seen as the child of Shiva and Parvati, Ganesha is the remover of obstacles. This print (1878–83) casts him as scribe to the composer of the *Mahabharata*.

### PARVATI
Parvati, who is shown placing a wedding garland on Shiva in this 19th-century painting, is a benevolent goddess associated with love and motherhood.

### SATI
According to one myth, Sati was Shiva's first wife; in this painting of *c.* 1865–75 he carries her corpse. After she died, she was reborn as Parvati.

### DURGA
Durga is a fearsome goddess, created by the gods to slay a demon against whom they were powerless. This 19th-century painting depicts her victory over Manisha.

**Venuses of Grimaldi**
*Discovered in the Balzi Rossi caves in Liguria, Italy, these Palaeolithic (Old Stone Age) Venus figurines depict the female form. Speculation that they represent goddesses has led many modern Pagans to adopt Venus figurines into their own practice.*

images were not set up to facilitate worship but were instead perceived as decorative artworks fit to adorn the gardens and palaces of the wealthy.

\* \* \*

The deities of those pre-Christian traditions once found in Europe, North Africa and West Asia have been particularly influential in the emergence of modern Paganism. Like the Neoplatonists before them, many modern Pagans adopt views close to monism or monotheism, even if they reject the Judeo-Christian God. The Temple of Set, founded in California, USA, in 1975, for example, heralds the ancient Egyptian god Set as the one true divinity, believing him responsible for setting humanity apart from other animals by gifting them a superior intellect. Although open to multiple interpretations, members of the Goddess movement typically talk of 'the Goddess' as a single entity, often modelling their portrayals of her on the mysterious Venus figurines produced by Palaeolithic (Old Stone Age) communities in Europe and Asia.

Also found among modern Pagans is duotheism, a belief in a complementary god and goddess. This was

*Pan and the Nymphs*, detail,
1st century
*Painted onto the wall of the
House of Jason at Pompeii,
Italy, this fresco shows the
horned god Pan accompanied
by three nymphs, one of
whom plays the lyre.*

the stance of many early Wiccans, whose theology revolved around a Horned God and a Mother Goddess. Theirs was a belief in the importance of a gendered polarity – the male and the female in balance – and they often held to the view advanced by British occultist Dion Fortune (1890–1946) that 'all gods are one God, and all goddesses are one Goddess'.

As the decades passed and social attitudes evolved, many modern Pagans felt more comfortable embracing an explicitly polytheistic worldview. Indeed, by the 2010s, some were preferring to be called 'Polytheists' rather than 'Pagans'. Often, they felt able to eclectically worship any deities who attracted them. Thus, there are people worshipping a personalized combination of entities drawn from, for example, ancient Egyptian, Norse and Hindu theologies. Other modern Pagans only venerate what they see as a single pantheon taken from a particular region, immersing themselves in the evidence for pre-Christian religion in that area.

While most deities worshipped by modern Pagans come from the non-Christian traditions of the Old World, some would probably not be immediately

## PROFILE
### NORSE GODS + GODDESSES

The Norse peoples of Scandinavia believed in a range of divinities whose stories were later written down largely by medieval Christian Icelanders. According to Norse mythology, these gods were divided among two groups, the Æsir and the Vanir, who were once at war before coming together as one. In addition to leaving their mark on placenames such as Odense in Denmark, the Norse gods have influenced artists including Norwegian painter Peter Nicolai Arbo, who created *The Wild Hunt of Odin* (1872, right). Three of Jakob Siggurdsson's illustrations from a manuscript of 1760 are shown below, alongside three of Arthur Rackham's illustrations from *The Rhinegold and the Valkyrie* (1910, below right).

*ODIN*
Chief of the Æsir, Odin is linked with diverse phenomena, from poetry to the dead.

*THOR*
The son of Odin, Thor is a god of thunder and lightning, wielder of his famous hammer.

*TYR*
Tyr is a god of sky, war and council, who lost his arm to the wolf Fenrir at Ragnarök.

*FRIGG*
Odin's wife Frigg is the Æsir's main goddess, possibly linked with womanhood and love.

*FREYJA*
A member of the Vanir, Freyja is a goddess of fertility and a guardian of the domestic arena.

*LOKI*
A trickster, Loki is an ambiguous character who both helps the gods and fathers their enemies.

recognizable to these ancient societies. The Horned God of Wicca, for example, is a composite character drawing on such deities as the Gaulish Cernunnos and the Greek Pan, as well as historical arguments that the horned Devil of the early modern imagination had been a surviving pre-Christian god. Another popular modern Pagan deity, the Green Man, similarly arises from the (since discredited) views of early 20th-century scholars that the foliate heads carved in medieval churches represented a surviving pre-Christian divinity.

Unlike their pre-Christian forebears, modern Pagans live in societies where the existence of supernatural beings is not taken for granted. While some Pagans do believe that their deities exist literally, others offer alternative explanations as to what the gods and goddesses are. Some Pagans are atheists or agnostics, taking the view that the deities are merely symbolic of the different facets of the human experience. In certain instances, they turn to Jungian psychology, perceiving these deity forms to be archetypes arising from the collective unconscious. There is, thus, considerable variation in modern Pagan understandings of theology.

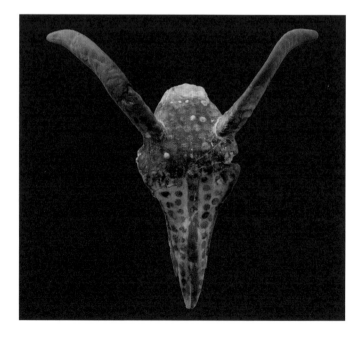

**Egyptian Bucranium,**
*c.* 1640–*c.* 1550 BC
*A bucranium is a decorative motif that denotes an ox killed as part of a religious sacrifice. Here, the bone and antlers are painted.*

**Modern Horned God**

*This modern reconstruction of a Celtic shrine adjacent to a natural spring features a timber antlered deity. It is located at the Castell Henllys Iron Age Village, a heritage attraction in Pembrokeshire, Wales. How widely venerated antlered deities actually were in Iron Age Europe is unclear.*

## PROFILE
YORUBA
*ORISHAS*

The *orishas* are the deities traditionally venerated by West Africa's Yoruba people and also by some of their descendants in the Americas. Each *orisha* is subservient to the creator divinity, usually called Olodumare. A key concept in Yoruba religion is that the *orishas* can possess their devotees, usually in a ceremonial context, and it is in this way that they regularly communicate with humanity. Carved female devotional figures are seen here at the shrine of Shango in Ede, Osun State, Nigeria.

### OBATALA
Often regarded as the father of the *orishas*, the white-clad Obatala is responsible for forming the first humans.

### ELEGUA
Elegua controls entrances, so in some traditions he must be approached before contact can be made with other *orishas*.

### OSHUN
Associated with the Nigerian river bearing her name, Oshun is an *orisha* of water, purity, sensuality and love.

### YEMANJÁ
One of the most prominent goddesses in Yoruba theology, Yemanjá is an *orisha* of the sea and a protector of women.

### SHANGO
Recognizable by his double-headed axe, Shango is a former human king who is associated with fire and lightning.

### IBEJI
The Ibeji are twin *orishas*, reflecting the various unusual associations that twins are thought to have in Yoruba culture.

# MYTHS + LEGENDS

KOJIKI, VOLUME I, SECTION 3

TRANS. BASIL HALL CHAMBERLAIN

> SO THE TWO DEITIES, STANDING UPON THE FLOATING BRIDGE OF HEAVEN, PUSHED DOWN THE JEWELLED SPEAR AND STIRRED WITH IT, WHEREUPON, WHEN THEY HAD STIFFED THE BRINE TILL IT WENT CURDLE-CURDLE, AND DREW THE SPEAR UP, THE BRINE THAT DRIPPED DOWN FROM THE END OF THE SPEAR WAS PILED UP AND BECAME AN ISLAND.

Through their myths and legends, societies put forward stories about their gods and goddesses, demons and heroes - stories that include the creation of the universe, epic wars and sometimes even the end of the world itself. Explaining why life and society are as they are or how humans can live in an appropriate manner, these narratives provide the basis for a rich selection of rituals, festivals and visual culture produced by communities across the world.

Communities that believe in a panoply of goddesses and gods have long devised rich and complex stories about their activities. These myths piece together into broader mythologies, often dealing with major questions regarding the origin of the cosmos and of humanity itself. Polytheistic cultures typically tell stories of human beings, among them epics of kings, warriors and witches, which are sometimes called 'legends' to differentiate them from the more cosmological narratives found in myth. Boundaries between myth and legend can, nevertheless, be considerably blurred, for all are part of each society's unique tradition of storytelling.

Scholars have long debated the purpose of myth. Some have insisted that its function is primarily psychological, for example to help people live out aspects of their unconscious minds. Others have argued that myth has more to do with society, offering explanations for why the world is as it is – why people get sick and die, or why an elite governs everybody else, for example – or providing a mental escape from the unpleasantness of the everyday. The characters appearing in mythical and legendary narratives can also offer exemplars designed to influence the behaviour of those who hear them, encouraging piety towards the gods. Myth is multifunctional, operating at different levels and in different ways.

For most of history, myths and legends were only passed down orally. Although literacy is now far more widespread, many societies still prefer to transmit their stories in a traditional oral fashion. This can result in variation, with different storytellers recounting different versions of the same mythological narrative. Passing down myths in oral form carries the risk of these stories being lost, often because of religious change. Despite coming from a literate culture, we, for example, know comparatively little about the mythological stories involving the gods and goddesses of ancient Egypt, because the Egyptians themselves rarely wrote down extended narratives. One of the Egyptian myths best known today – the story of how the goddess Isis pieced together the body parts of

‹ page 52
Herbert Draper, *The Lament for Icarus*, c. 1898
*In this scene from ancient Greek legend, Icarus escapes his imprisonment on Crete by flying away on manufactured wings, only to die after flying too close to the sun.*

**Gustave Moreau, *Oedipus and the Sphinx*, 1864**

*Moreau's Symbolist painting depicts a scene from ancient Greek legend in which Oedipus confronts the Sphinx, a monster that asks him a riddle and threatens to devour him if he answers incorrectly. The corpse at Oedipus's feet references the Sphinx's prior victims, who failed to answer his riddle.*

## DECODING
*THE*
*JUDGEMENT*
*OF PARIS*

In this painting from the 1630s, Flemish artist Peter Paul Rubens portrays a scene from Greek mythology. Here, Paris of Troy must give the golden apple to one of three goddesses – Athena, Aphrodite and Hera – whom he deems the most beautiful.

1. Athena
2. Aphrodite
3. Hera
4. The Golden Apple

5. Hermes
6. Paris of Troy
7. The Fury Alecto

her husband, the god Osiris, after they were scattered by his brother Set – has been handed down largely through a text produced not by an Egyptian but by Greek author Plutarch (46–*c.* 119), who wrote in the 1st or early 2nd century.

Some societies have produced written accounts of their myths, allowing them to be passed down in a more stable form. In 8th-century Japan, for example, the *Kojiki* and *Nihon Shoki* were written documents, both offering versions of a creation myth that explains how the divinities created Japan and its people. These stories describe how the kings of Japan were descended from the sun goddess Amaterasu, thus demonstrating the way in which myths often serve the political agendas of those who transmit and promote them.

Legendary narratives were also preserved in text, exemplified by the well-known *Iliad* and *Odyssey*. According to tradition, these two epic poems were composed by a blind Greek poet named Homer in the 8th or 7th century BC. The *Iliad* recounts the actions of Greek warriors during the Trojan War, while the *Odyssey* focuses on one of these figures, King Odysseus, and his attempts to return home to Ithaca after the conflict. While the protagonists of these stories are human, their efforts are often either thwarted or

Lawrence Alma-Tadema,
*A Reading from Homer*,
1885
*An ancient Greek youth
recites one of Homer's epic
poems to his contemporaries.*

assisted by various gods and goddesses. In the *Odyssey*,
for example, the sea god Poseidon repeatedly delays
Odysseus's journey in vengeance for the Ithacan king's
blinding of Poseidon's son, the cyclops Polyphemus.
Homer's epics thus reflect a complex interplay between
the world of mortals and that of divinities.

Polytheistic societies have also portrayed their
myths and legends in visual form or enacted them
through song, dance and theatre. The ancient Greek
playwrights, for example, often produced works
dealing with the deeds of both humanity and the gods.
Euripides' (*c.* 484–406 BC) play *The Bacchae*, written
in the 5th century BC, tells the tale of Dionysus, a god
associated with wine and religious ecstasy. In the play,
Dionysus arrives in the city of Thebes and encourages
the Thebans to worship him as part of a scheme to punish
the city's king, Pentheus, who had previously banned
Dionysian rites. Dionysus succeeds in building up a
frenzied group of worshippers who eventually tear
Pentheus limb from limb – a scene that various Greek
visual artists also featured in their work.

As innovative technologies expand the types of
media available, so people have adopted new methods
of telling religious stories. One of the central legendary
tales of modern Hinduism is that of the Kurukshetra
War, as told in an epic poem titled the *Mahabharata*
(*c.* 400 BC). This tale has been adapted across a wide

## DECODING
HOMERIC
HEROES

Although little is known about him, the blind poet Homer has long been regarded as the composer of the two best-known epic poems of ancient Greece: the *Iliad* and the *Odyssey*. Scenes from Homer's epics made it onto various artworks produced by the ancient Greeks, such as this terracotta *hydria* or water jug dating from *c.* 510 BC. The black figure painting by Exekias depicts Achilles and Ajax, warriors who fought in the Trojan War.

### ACHILLES
Charles-Antoine Coypel's *Fury of Achilles* (1737) shows the eponymous Greek warrior, the son of the king of Phthia, who was responsible for killing the Trojan prince Hector.

### HECTOR
In *Hector Bidding Farewell to Andromache* (1760), Adam Friedrich Oeser depicts the Trojan prince leaving for war. After Hector was killed, his body was paraded before the Trojans.

### AENEAS
Simon Vouet's painting *Aeneas and his Father Fleeing Troy* (1635) features a Trojan warrior who escaped his devastated city. Aeneas later became the protagonist of Virgil's *Aeneid*.

### ODYSSEUS
As described in the *Odyssey*, King Odysseus encountered many creatures on his return from the war, including sirens, as seen in *Ulysses and the Siren* by John William Waterhouse (1891).

### AGAMEMNON
Appearing here in Michel-Martin Drolling's *The Wrath of Achilles* (1810), Agamemnon was king of Mycenae. He led the Greeks against Troy before being murdered upon his return home.

### PATROCLUS
Gavin Hamilton's *Achilles Lamenting the Death of Patroclus* (c. 1763) shows Achilles beside himself with grief at the slaying of his close friend – an act that he avenged by killing Hector.

**Marc Pachow,**
*Rangi and Papa*
*This artwork depicts two key figures from traditional Māori myth: Papa, the Earth goddess, and Rangi, the sky god. In a cosmogony myth the two partners were forcibly separated, resulting in the division of earth and sky.*

array of different mediums, including paintings, sculptures, puppet shows and dances, but in the past century Indian cinema goers have also been able to enjoy this old story retold in a string of film adaptations. Like Homer's work, the *Mahabharata* deals primarily with the affairs of warrior men, but various divine beings feature too, most notably the god Krishna.

★ ★ ★

Perhaps the most common forms of myth deal with beginnings: how the world and humanity came to exist. One such creation myth is that found among the Māori of New Zealand. Bearing similarities with the myths of other Polynesian societies, it describes how the sky god Rangi and the Earth goddess Papa once clung closely to each other. Their children – the rest of the gods – were squashed between them, unable to move freely, and so they decided to separate their parents. They encouraged the god Tāne to take the form of a giant tree, forcibly pushing Rangi upward and away from Papa. Ever since, the two separated lovers have wept for one another, evidenced by the mists and the rain.

An alternative creation narrative is that outlined in the aforementioned *Kojiki* and *Nihon Shoki*. These Japanese texts relate how, at the beginning of time,

Nishikawa Sukenobu,
*The God Izanagi and Goddess Izanami*, 18th century
*This painting features a scene from Shinto's main cosmogony, in which the kami siblings Izanagi and Izanami observe the formation of an island in the sea.*

the heavens separated from the earth, after which the earliest spirits, or *kami*, appeared. Two of these, Izanagi and his sister Izanami, then took a spear and stirred the primordial seas, resulting in a coagulation of brine forming an island. The siblings proceeded to the land, where Izanami gave birth to more *kami*, dying in the process. On seeing the decay of his sister's body, Izanagi sought to purify himself by bathing in the sea, at which point more *kami* sprang from his body, including the sun *kami* Amaterasu, who ultimately appointed her grandson to rule over Japan.

Many societies also have myths about eschatology, the end of the world. One of the most dramatic eschatological myths is that of Ragnarök, a story from the Norse peoples of Scandinavia. Although the narrative is only recorded in 13th-century texts written by Icelandic Christians – and in this form might have been influenced by accounts of the Christian apocalypse – the appearance of scenes from Ragnarök in stone

## PROFILE
## THE TWELVE LABOURS OF HERCULES

The hero known as Hercules to the Romans and Heracles to the Greeks was one of the most popular figures in the legends of the Classical world. In Greek mythology, he was the son of

*THE NEMEAN LION*
The first of Hercules' tasks was to kill the Nemean lion. The beast was impervious to bladed weapons, so Hercules clubbed and strangled it.

*THE LERNAEAN HYDRA*
Hercules had to slay the serpentine Lernaean hydra. Every time one of its heads was severed, another would grow in its place.

*THE CERYNEIAN HIND*
For his third labour, Hercules was tasked with capturing the Ceryneian hind and bringing it to King Eurystheus at Mycenae.

*THE ERYMANTHIAN BOAR*
Hercules' fourth labour was to capture the Erymanthian boar, bind it in chains and then drag it back to Mycenae to present before King Eurystheus.

*THE AUGEAN STABLES*
Hercules had to clean the masses of dung from the Augean stables for his fifth task. To achieve this, he diverted a river through the building.

*THE STYMPHALIAN BIRDS*
Hercules next had to slay the man-eating Stymphalian birds, shooting several down with arrows that had been dipped in the hydra's blood.

the god Zeus and a mortal woman known as Alcmene, resulting in his quasi-divine status. Possessed of great strength, he was known for the series of labours he was forced to perform.

*THE CRETAN BULL*
A great bull was wreaking havoc on the island of Crete. For his seventh labour, Hercules was tasked with capturing it and bringing it to Mycenae.

*THE MARES OF DIOMEDES*
Hercules had to steal the wild man-eating mares owned by King Diomedes of Thrace, but ended up killing the monarch in the process.

*THE BELT OF HIPPOLYTA*
Next, Hercules had to retrieve the belt of Hippolyta, a queen of the Amazons, and give it to Princess Admete, daughter of Eurystheus.

*THE CATTLE OF GERYON*
For his tenth task, Hercules had to steal the cattle belonging to the monster Geryon, along the way defeating a two-headed guard dog.

*THE GOLDEN APPLES OF THE HESPERIDES*
Hercules had to steal the golden apples belonging to Zeus. These were kept by a group of nymphs called the Hesperides.

*CERBERUS*
For his final task, Hercules had to travel to the underworld, capture the multi-headed guard dog Cerberus and bring him back to King Eurystheus.

Emil Doepler, *Odin and Fenrir and Freyr and Surtr*, *c.* 1905
*In this book illustration, the gods Odin and Freyr fight monsters during the Ragnarök battle.*

Emil Doepler, *After Ragnarök*, *c.* 1905
*German artist Doepler depicts the world as it is reborn in the aftermath of Ragnarök.*

carvings suggests that this myth was once widespread among the pre-Christian Norse. The Ragnarök narrative holds that the world will face four great catastrophes: a three-year winter, a fire burning across the world, the sinking of the land into the sea, and then the eclipse of the sun, devoured by the giant wolf Fenrir. The gods will be faced by an army of their enemies, the *jötnar*, and the god Odin will die in battle with Fenrir. Thor will succeed in killing the mighty Midgard Serpent, but himself succumb to its poison. Ultimately, a blazing fire will then consume all and the world will be destroyed. Amid the ashes, however, a new world will arise from the sea.

The end of this myth suggests that the pre-Christian Norse may have had a cyclical view of the cosmos, a perspective known from other non-Abrahamic societies. Hindu scriptures known as *Puranas*, for example, relate how the cosmos undergoes a cycle of four *yugas*, or ages. Each age is deemed more degenerate than the last, with our present *Kali yuga* – in which humans have largely forgotten their religious duties to the gods – being the worst. It is because of this, many Hindus believe, that the god Vishnu will one day incarnate on Earth in the figure of Kalki, a warrior riding upon a white horse. According to this view, Kalki is destined to bring an end to the *Kali yuga*, purifying the cosmos and allowing the cycle to commence from the beginning again.

*Kali Attacking Nisumbha,*
*c. 1740*
In this painting, probably from
northern India, the ferocious
Hindu goddess Kali slays a green
asura (demon), Nisumbha. The
killing of asuras is a recurring
attribute of Hindu deities.

Many people who get involved in modern Paganism
recount having had a childhood fascination for myths
and legends. They, nevertheless, grow up in contexts
where scientific enquiry has offered its own accounts
of cosmogony and cosmology, and thus rarely believe
in the literal truth of ancient myth. Instead, they often
look upon such stories as sources of wisdom. Some
Heathens, or those who venerate the pre-Christian
deities of the Germanic-speaking peoples, for example,
see Ragnarök as a warning about the threats posed
by environmental degradation. Elsewhere, Pagans
have interpreted ancient myths in ways that have
personal resonance. For example, many gay and
bisexual practitioners have taken great interest in
myths that can be interpreted as portraying same-sex
relationships, such as the companionship of the hero
Gilgamesh and the 'wild man' Enkidu in the ancient
Mesopotamian *Epic of Gilgamesh.*

Building on the ideas of 19th and early 20th-century
scholars, some modern Pagans have turned to legends
and folklore recorded in Christian centuries in the

## PROFILE
THOR

Pictured here in Mårten Eskil Winge's *Thor's Fight with the Giants* (1872), Thor was the Norse god of thunder and lightning. Son of the god Odin and the giantess Jörð, he was a fierce fighter who wielded a dwarf-made hammer named Mjölnir. Between the 9th and 11th centuries, many Old Norse religionists wore pendants representing this hammer.

*KVINNEBY AMULET*
Discovered in Öland, Sweden, this 11th-century amulet displays runic script invoking the protection of Thor and his hammer.

*SACRIFICE TO ODIN*
This Viking Age rune stone from Gotland has been interpreted as depicting Thor alongside two other prominent Old Norse deities, Odin and Freyr.

*SKÅNE HAMMER*
From Skåne, Sweden, this silver Mjölnir is decorated with filigree. At the top is a bird of prey head, with a protruding beak and bulging eyes.

*AMULET*
Discovered at Rømersdal in Bornholm, Denmark, this 9th-century amulet of Mjölnir is made from silver. The upper ring shows how it was possibly worn on a cord around the neck.

*HEATHENRY PENDANT*
This contemporary copy of the Mjölnir pendant is worn by many Heathens – members of a modern Pagan religion venerating pre-Christian Germanic gods.

*EYRARLAND STATUE*
Discovered near Akureyri in Iceland, the Eyrarland Statue (*c.* AD 1000) has been interpreted as a depiction of Thor and his famous hammer and has been adopted by many modern Heathens.

**Julia Margaret Cameron,**
***Idylls of the King,* 1874**

*One of the foremost poets of Victorian Britain, Alfred, Lord Tennyson, was inspired by Arthurian legend and used it as the basis for his poetic cycle,* Idylls of the King, *first published in 1859. In 1874, he commissioned the photographer Julia Margaret Cameron to produce images to illustrate a republication of the work.*

hope of finding traces of earlier pre-Christian mythology. This has been the case, for example, among those searching for the myths of the ancient Slavic-speaking peoples in Eastern Europe and the ancient Celtic speakers in the West. It has often been argued that certain characters from medieval sources, including the Welsh *Mabinogion* and the Irish *Ulster Cycle*, were originally gods. Accordingly, these entities and their attendant stories have been absorbed into forms of modern Paganism. Both earlier scholars and modern Pagans have also looked for pre-Christian significance in the Arthurian legends, stories that arose in medieval Britain and that focus on King Arthur and the search for the Holy Grail. One of the best-known modern Pagan Druids in Britain, for example, names himself King Arthur, owns a sword called Excalibur and refers to his followers as the Loyal Arthurian Warband. For many Pagans, the fact that the Arthurian tales have been recorded in Christian contexts does not prevent them from being mined for imagery, symbolism and terminology for use in modern Pagan ritual contexts. Other Pagans have turned to more recent stories for inspiration, such as the fantasy works of (the Roman Catholic) J. R. R. Tolkien (1892–1973) or the science fiction stories of (the agnostic) Robert Heinlein (1907–88). The Church of All Worlds, a Pagan group established in the USA during the 1960s, for example, takes its name and basic structure from a fictional religion in Heinlein's novel *Stranger in a Strange Land* (1961).

In today's world, 'myth' can also denote a claim that is simply untrue, and there are certain narratives circulating in modern Pagan communities that both display the mythic power of creation stories and promote accounts about the past that most archaeologists and historians maintain are false. The best-known example is a claim that was especially popular among early Wiccans during the mid to late 20th century. They held that theirs was not a new religion, but an ancient one with roots among the hunter-gatherers of the Old Stone Age. If true, it would make Wicca the world's oldest surviving religion. According to this account, the ancient religion was persecuted throughout the Christian centuries – a period many Wiccans call the 'burning times' – with the Christian authorities demonizing its Horned God as the Devil and presenting its practitioners as Satanic witches. This was not a narrative that Wiccans invented themselves. Rather, it built upon ideas that were advanced during the 19th and early 20th centuries by scholars such as Jules Michelet (1798–1874) and Margaret Murray (1863–1963) as a means of trying to explain the 16th- and 17th-century witch trials. The early Wiccans had simply taken this historical theory, which had already been widely disseminated, and adopted it as their own origin myth during the 1950s. Only in the latter half of the 20th century, when historical investigation revealed that there had never been an organized religion of witches in Europe, did many Wiccans acknowledge that theirs was a new religion, albeit one inspired by historical sources.

Another modern Pagan claim is that which American scholar Cynthia Eller (b. 1958) called the 'myth of matriarchal prehistory'. Popular among the Goddess movement, this was the belief that humanity had been female-centred for most of prehistory, devoted to the worship of goddesses and living in harmony with the Earth. This account holds that this halcyon situation ended when patriarchal forces violently assumed power in *c.* 3000 BC, introducing male-dominated governance and the centrality of male gods. As with the Wiccan tale of the 'burning times', this narrative owed much to the notions of earlier academics, especially those of Lithuanian-American archaeologist Marija Gimbutas (1921–94), which various Pagans then adopted and imbued with spiritual significance. However, as scholars such as Eller noted, this 'myth' relies on a highly selective and ideologically charged reading of archaeological evidence and has not kept up with developing understandings of European prehistory.

Regardless of whether or not such narratives recount past events accurately, they offer many Pagans a meaningful guide for understanding their own place in the world. In this way, they act much like the traditional myths and legends of other non-Abrahamic religions.

**Hittite Woman and Child**     *Dating from the 14th or 13th century BC, this miniature gold sculpture was cast using the lost-wax technique. It is attributed to the Hittite people of Anatolia and was possibly intended as an amulet to be worn around the neck. The seated female figure may be a goddess, with her headdress representing the sun.*

# 3

# NUMINOUS NATURE

O, DAUGHTER OF LATONA,
GREATEST CHILD OF GREAT
JOVE, WHOSE MOTHER
GAVE BIRTH NEAR THE
DELIAN OLIVE, MISTRESS
OF MOUNTAINS AND
GREEN WOODS AND
LONELY GLADES AND
SOUNDING RIVERS.

CATULLUS

'SONG TO DIANA', POEMS, 34

Humans have long perceived the presence of
their deities in the fabric of the material world
itself. Rivers, lakes and springs, trees, rocks and
mountains all have been perceived as sacred
places, representing either the abode of spirits
and divinities or the very personification of
these entities themselves. Even in our world of
urbanized sprawl and grand human-built temples,
many communities continue to cherish these
natural places as being especially sacred.

arly Christians believed that one of the pagans' great errors was that they worshipped God's creation, rather than God himself. Ever since, many Christians have been especially concerned about people conducting rituals at rocks, rivers, springs and trees. In early 11th-century England, for example, Wulfstan (d. 1023), the Archbishop of York, lamented that people were still worshipping at trees and springs, maintaining that this was idol worship inspired by the Devil. Although they disapproved, Christians such as Wulfstan recognized that many communities perceive an innate sacredness in natural places and things. For these people, divinity is not intrinsically transcendent or separate from material reality, but rather can be embodied within the world itself.

Having inherited Christian frameworks for understanding the non-Abrahamic world, many early scholars of religion took a dismissive view of communities that sacralize the natural landscape, labelling it 'primitive' behaviour. One of the early scholars who tried to understand these activities was 19th-century British anthropologist Edward Tylor (1832–1917). He coined the term 'animism', by which he meant a belief that inanimate objects possess a supernatural spirit. Later scholars largely rejected this concept as too judgmental and derogatory, although some sought to rehabilitate the term. The 'new animism' describes an approach to the world in which humans seek to live in a relational way with other entities, whether they be animals, plants, rocks or non-corporeal spirits. This is common to many of the religions that Christians have labelled 'pagan', reflecting that religious activity is, for many people, fundamentally about creating and maintaining healthy relationships with the world around them.

* * *

The sacralization of natural phenomena is found in many ancient societies. Among the Greeks, temples were sometimes built inside pre-existing groves of trees that were sacred to a particular deity. One example is the temple of the god Poseidon, positioned within a

<page 74
**Meoto Iwa**
*The Meoto Iwa, or Wedded Couple Rocks, stand off the coast of Ise, Japan, at the Futami Okitama shrine. A shimenawa rope tied between them indicates their role as the home of a kami spirit.*

**Katsushika Hokusai,**
***Roben Waterfall at Oyama***
***in Sagami Province, c. 1827***

*In Shinto, purifying the body with water is typically undertaken before approaching a kami's abode, with waterfalls regarded as ideal locations for such ablution. In this print, pilgrims purify themselves on the way to the Aburi shrine on Mount Oyama.*

grove on the Greek island of Kalaureia. Trees, rivers and other natural landscape features were also perceived as the abode of supernatural entities, the nymphs, often portrayed as young women. Greco-Roman writers claimed that societies further north in Europe similarly revered groves, with medieval Christian accounts supporting the existence of sacred trees among northern peoples. In the early 8th century, English missionary Saint Boniface (*c.* 675–*c.* 754) reportedly discovered and cut down the 'Oak of Jupiter', venerated by a community in Germany. Several decades later, the Frankish king Charlemagne (*c.* 747–814) reputedly oversaw the felling of Irminsul, a timber pillar venerated by the Saxons. In the 11th century, German writer Adam of Bremen (*c.* 1040–1081/85) complained that worshippers at Uppsala, Sweden, drowned human victims in a spring next to a tree that remained green all year round.

Exactly how Europe's pre-Christian societies interpreted these sacred trees remains unclear. Some may have been associated with belief in a world tree. While such ideas are found in various communities around the world, the best-known European example is Yggdrasil, a cosmic ash tree in Norse mythology, under the roots of which humanity was believed to live. While Christian theology offered less space for these

Pierre Puvis de Chavannes, *The Sacred Grove, Beloved of the Arts and Muses*, 1884
*In this painting, the French artist presents his imagined variant of an ancient Greek sacred grove populated by the muses.*

sacralized facets of the natural world, many springs, trees and stones remained important for Europe's Christians. During the Middle Ages, these landscape features were often connected to the veneration of saints – and for that reason were also denounced as 'pagan' by Protestant Reformers. Today, wooded groves remain sacred sites for many non-Abrahamic communities. Followers of the traditional religion of the Mari people in Russia, for example, meet for communal rituals devoted to their gods in sacred groves called *küsoto*. Nigeria also has sacred groves, the best known of which is at Osun-Osogbo. Associated with Osun, a fertility *orisha* deity of the Yoruba people, the Osun-Osogbo grove comprises forty separate shrines scattered across one of southern Nigeria's last surviving areas of primary high forest. Many artworks now decorate the area, demarcating it as a special place.

Individual plants can also be thought of as having sacred significance. In Amazonia, ritual specialists from both indigenous and mestizo communities engage in visionary experiences in which they communicate with the spirits of different plants so as to learn about their healing capabilities. These experiences are often facilitated by consuming plants that induce psychoactive effects, most famously those ingested as part of the brew *ayahuasca*.

The sacralization of the natural world is also very evident in Hinduism, where many natural features are

## PROFILE
SACRED
TREES

Many non-Abrahamic societies have regarded certain trees as important, seeing them as manifestations of the cosmos, the home of indwelling deities or the physical manifestation of a divinity itself. Dating from the 1620s, this artwork by Italian sculptor Gian Lorenzo Bernini depicts a scene from Classical mythology in which the nymph Daphne transforms into a tree to escape the amorous interests of the god Apollo.

*OAK OF DONAR*
According to medieval
hagiographies, the English
missionary Saint Boniface cut
down the sacred Oak of Donar
in Hesse, Germany.

*IRMINSUL*
In the 8th century, Charlemagne
ordered the destruction of
Irminsul, a large timber pillar
sacred to the pre-Christian
Saxons.

*SACRED BANYAN TREE*
In India (as here, at a shrine
in Gaya, Bihar), certain banyan
trees are regarded as the
manifestation or dwelling
of Hindu deities.

*SHIMENAWA*
In Japanese Shinto, trees
believed to have an indwelling
*kami* spirit are identified by
a rope, the *shimenawa*, hung
around their trunk.

*TREE OF LIFE*
This complex stele from Izapa,
Mexico, depicts a tree that may
evidence a pre-Christian
Mesoamerican belief in a cosmic
tree of life.

*RITUAL OF OAK
AND MISTLETOE*
In this painting by Henri-Paul
Motte (1900), druids ceremonially
collect mistletoe from an oak tree
on the sixth day of the moon.

considered to be either the abode, or *vas*, of a deity, or the deity's physical embodiment itself, a *svarupa*. Many Hindus, for example, regard the Himalayan mountain Kailash as the abode of the god Shiva and sometimes identify it as Meru, the mountain that forms the *axis mundi* around which the world revolves in Hindu cosmology. From the Himalayas emerges the River Ganges, seen as a goddess who flows from Shiva's hair and in whose waters pilgrims bathe as a form of spiritual purification. Across South Asia, numerous trees – especially those of the pipal species – are regarded as a *svarupa* or *vas*. Many can be identified by the red cord tied around their trunks and the offerings placed about their roots. Rocks can also become objects of Hindu veneration. These include the oval or sometimes phallic-shaped *lingam* stones associated with Shiva and the *shalagrams* found in Nepal's Gandaki River, revered as *svarupas* of the god Vishnu.

Other facets of the South Asian landscape are associated not with any of the major deities of the Hindu pantheon but instead with lesser, localized

**The Old Pine Tree of Karasaki, c. 1901–07**
The vast pine tree depicted on this postcard is located in the village of Karasaki, near Lake Biwa, Japan. Shinto encourages respect for many trees, sometimes presenting them as the homes of indwelling kami.

entities. Across rural areas, trees are often connected with *yakshas*, pot-bellied spirits that can be either mischievous or benevolent, while pools and springs are commonly linked to snake-spirits called *nagas*. Offerings are left for these less powerful deities, sometimes in the hope of propitiating them and preventing them from becoming a nuisance, or alternatively to seek their assistance in dealing with the issues facing rural communities.

Links between spirits and the landscape can be seen in Japanese Shinto. Here, deities known as *kami* are believed to be capable of residing within material objects. These objects are termed *shintai* and include both natural and manufactured items. When natural landscape features are perceived in this way, they will often be demarcated with material culture that sets them apart: a tree or rock perceived as a *shintai* will, for example, often be marked out by a *shimenawa*, or twisted straw rope, hung upon it. These Japanese ideas about spirits residing in the natural environment have been popularized internationally through films such as Studio Ghibli's *My Neighbor Totoro* (1988) and *Princess Mononoke* (1997), both of which draw liberally on Japanese folklore.

## PROFILE
SACRED
ROCKS +
MOUNTAINS

Rocky outcrops in the landscape, most notably mountains, regularly inspire human awe. Many societies have deemed such places to be sacred, associating them with particular deities, key events in creation myths or core locations in the cosmos – exemplified by the depiction of the mythological Mount Meru in this 14th-century Chinese *mandala*. Sacred mountains can attract pilgrims who ascend them and leave offerings. They also serve as settings for important rituals or may be left intentionally unsullied by human presence.

*MOUNT FUJI*
This 19th-century print by Hiroshige depicts Mount Fuji, Japan. In Shinto, Fuji is thought to be inhabited by a *kami* named Konohanasakuya-hime.

*MOUNT KAILASH*
In Hindu belief, Mount Kailash in the Himalayas, pictured in this *thangka* (*c.* 1500), is the home of Shiva, and as a result attracts thousands of pilgrims every year.

*MOUNT OLYMPUS*
The ancient Greeks believed that the main deities, the Twelve Olympians, lived atop Mount Olympus, which is depicted in this fresco of 1819–20.

*ULURU*
Located in Australia's Northern Territory, Uluru is sacred for the local Pitjantjatjara people, who oppose climbing it and instead perform rituals in nearby caves.

*EXTERNSTEINE*
Speculation about pre-Christian ritual use has attracted modern Pagans to this prominent rocky sandstone outcrop in Germany's Teutoburg Forest.

*HELGAFELL*
According to one medieval saga, Iceland's early pre-Christian settlers regarded the mountain of Helgafell as being sacred to Thor, a god of thunder and lightning.

*From a villa in Sentinum, Italy, this Roman floor mosaic depicts Aion, the god of eternity, alongside the reclining Earth Mother goddess Terra Mater.*

> Gaia, c. 730
*Although this fresco was created for a Muslim household, many archaeologists believe that it depicts Gaia, the Greek Earth Mother goddess. It was painted within an Umayyad palace, the Qasr al-Hayr al-Gharbi in Syria.*

The notion of spirits inhabiting stones is a recurring feature in the traditional religion of West Africa's Yoruba people and also in the traditions that were formed largely by Yoruba communities in the Americas, such as Brazilian Candomblé and Cuban Santería. Here, the deities, known as *orishas*, are thought capable of inhabiting small stones, sometimes called *otanes*. Each of the *orishas* is associated with a particular type of stone; in Cuba, for example, pebbles from the sea are regarded as being the personification of Yemaya, a goddess of the ocean. A selection of these stones will typically be collected inside a vessel and housed in the sanctum of a temple. There, practitioners will 'feed' them by placing offerings, often including animal blood, either upon or in front of them.

While small portable objects such as stones can be regarded as representations of a deity, so Earth itself can be interpreted as divine. In ancient Greece, the goddess Gaia was an embodiment of Earth, and it was via her relationship with the sky god Ouranos that the Olympian deities ultimately descended. In the traditional religions of the Māori, Papa is the Earth Mother goddess and, like her Greek counterpart, is paired with a sky god, Rangi. Among traditional Andean cultures, the goddess Pachamama plays a similar role, and receives a range of different offerings, including animal sacrifices. Across the world, Earth is repeatedly deified in female rather than male form, suggesting a widespread conceptual link between motherhood

*Statuettes of foxes, known as* kitsune, *are commonly found at Shinto* jinja *(shrines) that are devoted to Inari, a* kami *of rice cultivation who takes both male and female forms. These examples are at Kyoto, the city that is home to the Fushimi Inari-taisha, a major* jinja *devoted to Inari.*

and the land on which people live. In regarding Earth itself as a divine being, it has been argued that these communities are more ideologically invested in a sustainable lifestyle than those, like followers of Abrahamic religions, who regard the planet as a profane creation.

Animals also play a prominent role in many non-Abrahamic religions. Cows are famously regarded as sacred by Hindus, serving as symbols of the gods' benevolence. Many Hindu deities are themselves associated with a particular animal, regarded as their *vahana,* or vehicle. The elephant-headed god Ganesh, for example, rides upon a rat, while the god Shiva is carried on the back of the bull Nandi. Similar associations between deities and particular animals can be seen in Shinto, where the best-known example is the *kitsune*, white foxes linked to Inari, a highly popular *kami* spirit associated with rice cultivation. In recorded Norse mythology, the god Odin is assisted by his two ravens, Huginn and Muninn, while the goddess Freyja rides a carriage pulled by cats. Animals can also be seen as having links to human beings. Prior to Christian and Soviet repressions, the peoples of North and Central Asia commonly believed that many of their ritual specialists were assisted by spirit animals. Among Turkic-speaking groups around Minusinsk in Russia, for example, frogs commonly took on this role. Animals could also symbolize human communities,

*GANGES*
In Hindu belief, the Ganges springs from the hair of Shiva and is often personified as a goddess, as pictured here.

*YAMUNA*
In this painting of *c.* 1770 Krishna plays with three of his eternal devotees, *gopis*, in the Yamuna, a tributary of the Ganges.

*NILE*
The Nile was crucial to the ancient Egyptians. This *c.* 1400 BC wall painting depicts the papyrus plants and animals living there.

## PROFILE
### SACRED
### WATERS

Across the world, many communities have regarded bodies of water as sacred places. Rivers, lakes, ponds, springs and wells have all been incorporated into religious beliefs and practices, perceived as the homes of a god or goddess, the physical embodiment of a deity itself or a suitable place in which to deposit offerings to divine beings. As barriers between the land and underwater realms, these liminal zones are often treated with particular respect. They have also evoked artistic interest, as in John William Waterhouse's *Hylas and the Nymphs* (1896), which draws on a tale from Classical myth.

*OSUN*
In Yoruba religion, Nigeria's Osun River is associated with an *orisha* deity of the same name. A statue in her honour is pictured here.

*SACRED CENOTE*
In pre-Christian Mesoamerica, votive offerings were often cast into cenotes (water-filled sinkholes) such as this.

*DEVIL'S POOL*
According to a Yidiny legend, Devil's Pool in Queensland, Australia, is haunted by the ghost of a drowned woman.

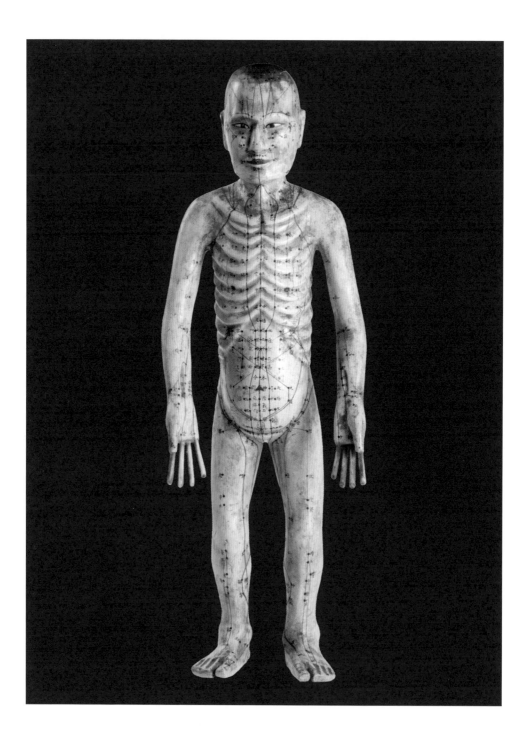

**Acupuncture Figurine**

*This East Asian figurine is marked with acupuncture points and was used to teach those learning acupuncture. Traditional Chinese acupuncture treatments rely on a belief in chì or qì as a cosmic force flowing through the body. Needles are inserted into the body at various points on the pathways of chì or qì.*

*pages 90–91*
**Kumbh Mela Festival**
*During the Kumbh Mela festival, which is held at the city of Prayagraj, India, every twelve years, Hindu pilgrims immerse themselves in waters where three sacred rivers – the Ganges, Yamuna and Saraswati - meet.*

such as clans. Bears, beavers and eagles all make regular appearances on the totem poles of the Pacific Northwest, often in their capacity as heraldic images referencing the particular clan responsible for the pole's creation. Many Christian missionaries ordered these poles to be destroyed, on the mistaken belief that they were 'idols' whom the indigenous peoples worshipped.

Another recurring feature of many non-Abrahamic religions is a belief that the natural world and everything in it are imbued with a cosmic force. In the traditional religion of North America's Lakota people, this force is called *wakan*, while among the Yoruba a similar energy is termed *ashe* and in Chinese religions it is *qi* or *chi* that imbues the physical universe. Although there are differences in how these societies view such forces, a common belief is that the energy sources can be manipulated to assist humans, for example in healing rituals. For followers of these religions, such forces help to form an interconnected web throughout the universe that humans must navigate to achieve a successful life.

\* \* \*

Some of the earliest modern Pagans were aware that Christians had long associated what they called 'paganism' with veneration of the natural world. However, it was only in the 1970s that the connection between modern Paganism and nature became far more explicit, as practitioners, especially in the USA, began referring to their own beliefs as 'nature religion' or 'earth religion'. This shift accompanied, and was almost certainly influenced by, the growth of modern environmental activism and the celebration of the first Earth Day in 1970.

By the closing decades of the 20th century, it was common for modern Pagans to express concerns about human destruction of the natural environment. Indeed, environmentalist sentiments are perhaps one of the only values shared across the modern Pagan milieu, which is otherwise divided among various left- and right-wing ideologies. For many

## PROFILE
## SACRED
## PLANTS

Plants are an important part of many non-Abrahamic religious traditions. In some cases, they are appreciated for their healing capabilities, reflecting the interconnection between the religious and medicinal spheres in many societies. Elsewhere, certain plants may be valued because they are thought to be favoured by the gods. A common idea is that different plant species each have their own particular spirit, one with whom certain individuals can communicate. In many cases, there are rituals associated with the harvesting of these plants, often involving giving something back to the plant in return for what is taken.

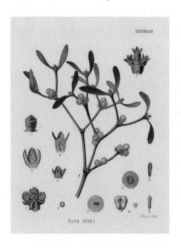 

### MISTLETOE
According to Roman writer Pliny, the druids of Western Europe regarded mistletoe as a sacred plant and harvested it using a golden sickle during a larger ritual requiring the sacrifice of bulls. Pliny wrote that the druids then used the mistletoe to impart fertility and cure people from any poisonings.

### SAKAKI
In Japan, the *Cleyera japonica* is commonly known as sakaki, a term denoting its sacred character. Practitioners of Shinto will often add zigzag strips of paper or cloth to a sakaki branch to create a *tamagushi*, which will then be given as an offering to the *kami* or used as an amulet.

### AYAHUASCA

In much of Amazonia, the vine *Banisteriopsis caapi* is a common ingredient in the production of a brew known as *ayahuasca*. This brew is ingested by people seeking visionary experiences in which they contact spirits, including those of the plants themselves.

### PEYOTE

A small cactus native to parts of Mexico and Texas, peyote contains the psychoactive substance mescaline. Its use in ceremonies spread among various Indigenous American communities during the 20th century, promoted by groups such as the Native American Church.

### SAGE

Among several indigenous communities in the North American Plains, sage has various religious uses. It is given as an offering to spirits and is burnt to purify a space, for example in preparation for ritual. The latter practice has been adopted by groups other than Indigenous Americans, generating some controversy.

< Oberon Zell-Ravenheart,
*Millennial Gaia*, 1998
*This sculpture of the Earth
Mother goddess is probably
the most popular image of this
entity among modern Pagans.*

> Oberon Zell-Ravenheart,
*Diana*
*Aimed at a modern Pagan
market, this sculpture of
the Roman goddess Diana
references the deity's lunar
associations.*

Pagans, this concern has not resulted in much practical action, but other adherents have become active radical environmentalists. In the USA, various modern Pagans joined groups such as Earth First! during the 1980s, while in Britain they took part in direct action protests against expanding road construction in the 1990s. These individuals came to be called 'Eco-Pagans' and closely interwove their religious commitments with their environmentalist activism. For them, defending planet Earth was a sacred duty.

The growing association between modern Paganism and nature religion also impacted Pagan visual cultures. The Green Man, a foliate head that readily evokes humanity's interconnection with the natural world, became an increasingly common image among modern Pagans in the late 20th century, found in Pagan magazines and at Pagan Pride marches. Meanwhile, the ancient Greek goddess Gaia was widely adopted as a Mother Earth figure, famously portrayed as a mother cradling Earth as her unborn child in a sculpture by Oberon Zell-Ravenheart (b. 1942), a prominent American Pagan involved in the formation of the Church of All Worlds.

August Malmström,
*Dancing Fairies*, 1866
*The Swedish painter drew on
his country's folklore to depict
ethereal* älvalek *floating over
a watery landscape.*

Images such as these reflect a modern Pagan perception of Earth as a deity itself, a belief akin to that found among indigenous Andean and Māori cultures. However, many modern Pagans also believe in a wider array of spirits inhabiting different facets of the landscape. Among modern Druids, for example, rituals taking place in the open air will often involve prayers directed to the 'spirit of the place', a term taken from the Latin *genius loci*. Many Pagans connect these landscape spirits to supernatural beings from European folklore – among them fairies, elves, gnomes, goblins and dragons – and some recount personal encounters with such entities. Whereas much of the older recorded folklore presents fairies and related beings as dangerous, many modern Pagans look upon them positively as 'nature spirits' or 'elementals', and in a few cases – as in the tradition of Fairy Wicca – accord them a prominent place in spiritual activities. For some more environmentally active Pagans, these supernatural entities can be seen as allies in combating human degradation of the natural environment.

## DECODING
FAIRIES

Throughout history, people across Europe have believed that humanity shares its world with supernatural beings. These entities live in many environments, from mines to rivers and woods – as portrayed in Edward Robert Hughes' *Midsummer Eve* (*c.* 1908). These creatures often held an uncertain place in Christian cosmology, but have found a more comfortable role as 'nature spirits' in modern Paganism.

ELVES
Alfons Mucha's *Elf with Iris Flowers* (*c.* 1886–90) is an interpretation of a type of entity found in various Germanic language societies. Elves are often characterized as mischievous.

TROLLS
John Bauer's depiction of a troll family from 1915 evokes these communal yet dim beings from Scandinavian lore – creatures that are often hostile to men and turn to stone in the daylight.

GOBLINS
Shown in Arthur Rackham's illustration for *Goblin Market* (*c.* 1933), goblins have appeared in European traditions since the Middle Ages, typically as small troublesome creatures.

LEPRECHAUNS
John Petts' 1908 illustration depicts a leprechaun, a solitary entity from Irish lore. In the 20th century, it became an internationally recognized symbol of Ireland itself.

GNOMES
Swiss alchemist Paracelsus introduced his idea of gnomes in the 16th century. The underground creatures are portrayed here by Arthur Rackham.

DOMOVOY
Depicted in Sergei Chekhonin's *The Peasant and the Domovoy* (1922), the domovoy is a household spirit that appears in the lore of Slavic language societies.

PART TWO

# RITUAL

1

SACRED SITES

2

WITCHCRAFT

3

ORACLES + DIVINATION

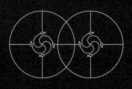

/ˈrɪtʃʊəl/noun

*A ceremony consisting of actions performed to a prescribed order.*

# Sacred Sites

HOMER, *ILIAD*, BOOK I

IF I HAVE EVER DECKED YOUR
TEMPLE WITH GARLANDS, OR
BURNED YOUR THIGH-BONES
IN FAT OF BULLS OR GOATS,
GRANT MY PRAYER, AND
LET YOUR ARROWS AVENGE
THESE MY TEARS.

TRANS. SAMUEL BUTLER

Most of the world's religions have certain spaces
or sites that are favoured for religious activities.
For many non-Abrahamic traditions, these places
are often regarded as innately sacred, locations
where a deity resides or manifests before their
worshippers in material form. At these sites,
people assemble to pay homage to particular
gods and goddesses, typically by providing them
with offerings or gifts to express their devotion,
fulfil a vow or seek divine favour.

**N**atural landscape features such as trees, rivers, pools and mountains have been sites of religious significance for millennia, but today many non-Abrahamic communities set aside certain buildings as sacred places. Often generically labelled 'temples', these structures are typically envisioned as places where deities reside or manifest in physical form. Thus, they are deemed appropriate locations where worshippers can approach powerful divine beings.

In some cases, sacred places combine natural and human-built components. This is perhaps most evident at the *jinja* (shrines) in Japanese Shinto. These usually take the form of an open-air enclosure that is separated from the profane world by distinctive gateways known as *torii*. The *jinja* may contain natural features such as rocks and trees, some of which will be regarded as possessing indwelling *kami* spirits, and they will typically be accompanied by several timber buildings. The main building is termed the *honden* and it is here that the important *kami* of that particular *jinja* is believed to reside, often inside a concealed object. Worshippers do not usually enter the *honden* itself, but stand outside, offering their prayers to the *kami* within.

This arrangement would have been somewhat familiar to the ancient Greeks. In ancient Greece, a sacred sanctuary was called a *temenos* and, like the Japanese *jinja*, would often include natural features such as wooded groves. Over time, it became increasingly common for a temple to be constructed within the *temenos*, serving as a *foci* for worship. By the 7th century AD, these temples generally followed a standard architectural form: a rectangular stone structure was flanked by external columns, with a prominent image of the deity at the centre. As with the *jinja*, worshippers would often remain outside the temple, making offerings at an external altar. This architectural style was later adopted by the Romans and gained widespread use throughout southern Europe.

Rather than combining natural and artificial elements in the manner of a *temenos* or *jinja*, the Hindu temple, or *mandir*, seeks to imitate natural forms, its roof peaking to resemble a mountain. At the heart of

<page 101
Elihu Vedder, *The Pleiades*, 1885
*In Greek mythology, the Pleiades were the seven daughters of the titan Atlas and the sea-nymph Pleione, from whom their name derives.*

< page 102
José Rico Cejudo, *The Vestals*, c. 1890
*In ancient Rome, the Vestal Virgins were the priestesses of the goddess Hera. During their term of service, they were required to remain celibate.*

**Athenian Temples**

*Three sets of black-and-white photographs depict ancient temples in Athens, Greece, as they appeared in the 1900s. They show the Erechtheion, designed by the architect Mnesikles (top, 1901), the Temple of Hephaestus, surrounded by a single row of columns (middle, 1907) and the Parthenon, part of a rebuilding programme led by Pericles (bottom, 1902).*

## PROFILE
*JINJA*

In the Japanese religion of Shinto, shrines are known as *jinja* and are seen as places where the *kami* spirits reside. Enclosures that juxtapose buildings alongside open-air spaces, the *jinja* have many recognizable features. As regular sites in the Japanese landscape, they have often appeared in artworks, such as this early 17th-century painted folding screen, *The Torii Gate of Gion Shrine*. Unlike churches and mosques, the shrines do not hold weekly services but are, nevertheless, visited regularly by Shinto's adherents, who come to give prayers and offerings to the *kami* enshrined there.

**TORII**

The *torii* archway marks the entrance to the *jinja*, they are also a distinctive symbol of Japanese culture more broadly. This example is on Itsukushima island. While different styles exist, most are painted vermilion.

**HONDEN**

This is the *honden* (the *jinja's* main sanctuary) of the Taiyin Mausoleum in Nikko. Typically, the *honden* is where the main *kami* of that shrine is believed to live, often inside a concealed object such as a sword or a mirror.

**HAIDEN**

The *haiden* is a place for worshippers to both pray and give offerings, which can include food, drink and monetary gifts, to the *kami* enshrined at that particular *jinja*. This is the *haiden* of Kyoto's Shikichi-jinja Shrine.

**BETSUGU**

Many *jinja* enshrine not one *kami* but several. The *betsugu*, also known as a *hekku*, is a subsidiary shrine in which *kami* other than those in the *honden* reside. This is the *betsugu* of the Ise Grand Shrine in Mie.

**CHINJU NO MORI**

Many *jinja* are situated in areas of woodland, referred to as *chinju no mori*. These can vary widely in size, sometimes covering whole swathes of a mountainside, as in this example in the mountains of Hanamaki.

**KOMAINU**

The *komainu* are a pair of stone lion-like beasts who guard the entrance to the *jinja* and keep out malevolent spirits. One will often have its mouth open, the other closed. This example comes from Itsukushima island.

‹ *pages 106–7*
**Hobbe Smith,** *Floralia,*
**1898**
*Celebrated in ancient Rome*
*each April, Floralia was a*
*festival celebrated in honour*
*of the goddess Flora.*

**Hindu Temples**
*In these two 17th-century*
*Indian paintings, Hindus*
*undertake* puja *(worship) of*
*their deity at a* mandir *(temple).*

the interior is the *garbhagriha* (womb chamber), an
inner sanctum that represents a cave. The main image
of the deity is kept here. Hindus will often encircle
the *mandir* before entering, and then perambulate the
interior before approaching the centre and presenting
their offerings to the enshrined deity.

The idea of a building being set aside exclusively for
worship is not found in all non-Abrahamic communities.
Among the Māori, for example, spiritual significance
is invested in the *wharenui*, a traditionally timber hall
located inside an enclosure known as a *marae*. This is,
nevertheless, not a place of worship in the same sense
as a *mandir*. Used for a range of social functions, the
*wharenui* is conceptualized as a material manifestation
of the Māori's ancestors, with different parts of the
building associated with different parts of the ancestral
body. Similarly, a timber longhouse is used for key
communal rituals among many indigenous societies
in the Pacific Northwest. Communities gather at the
longhouse to feast and to engage in ceremonial songs
and dances, for example at the annual First Salmon
festival. The way in which these buildings serve various

functions demonstrates how, for many people, religion is not disconnected from other areas of life.

In some societies, it is common for people to set aside a space in their home for the worship of deities. Among the ancient Romans, household altars were often devoted to the *penates*, spirits who protected parts of the house, and the *lares*, entities who protected the family. Household shrines are also common in modern Hinduism and Shinto, allowing worshippers to easily honour their deities daily. Another recurring feature of non-Abrahamic Asian religions is the altar set aside for deceased ancestors. In Chinese culture, for example, paper money is ritually burnt at these altars, thereby gifting it to the ancestors for use in the afterlife.

\* \* \*

Many religions emphasize the building of reciprocal relationships with deities and other non-human entities. To this end, it is common for adherents to give offerings to such beings at locations set apart as sacred. The nature of these gifts, however, varies widely, with food and drink perhaps being the most common choices.

**Sacrificial Reliefs**
*Two Roman reliefs depict sacrificial rituals. One dates from the 2nd century and shows Emperor Marcus Aurelius and his family sacrificing in thanks for military victories (left); the other is a 1st-century scene from the Temple of Vespasian in Pompeii, Italy (right).*

This suggests that, like humans, the deities require or desire sustenance. Often, worshippers share in this food, sometimes consuming that which has already been offered to a divinity. In Hinduism, food offered to the gods becomes *prasāda*: having been blessed by the divine, it thus bears spiritual benefit for whomever eats it. Other offerings, such as flowers or incense, reveal an attempt to beautify the environment around the divinity. Song and dance may also be provided for the deity's entertainment, with some wealthier Hindu *mandirs* able to employ entertainers full time.

In many societies, sacrificed animals form a key part of religious offerings. Among the ancient Greeks and Romans, species often selected for sacrifice included sheep, goats, pigs and poultry, with ox regarded as a special offering. The animal was led to an outdoor altar in front of the temple, where it was killed – often by having its throat cut. Blood was collected and then splattered onto the altar, after which the carcass was butchered. The inner organs were removed and burnt on a fire upon the altar, the smoke regarded as an offering to the deities. The rest of the meat was then cooked and eaten by those in attendance.

Several religions place less emphasis on the meat and instead regard the blood as centrally important. In Yoruba traditional religion and the American traditions based upon it, blood is seen to contain the cosmic

**Sun Dance Ritual**
*The Sun Dance is part of the traditional religions of various Plains societies. These photographs show two Cheyenne men pledged to perform the dance (left, c. 1910) and a Crow man engaged in it (right, c. 1908).*

force, or *ashe*, and it is this that is consumed by the *orisha* deities. Often, the animal is sacrificed in the temple itself, in the direct presence of the *orishas*. Elsewhere, emphasis is placed on avoiding the presence of blood in offerings. In Shinto, for example, fish and occasionally other meats are given to the *kami*, but the animal is not sacrificed directly before the deity. In the Shinto view, the shedding of blood is a source of impurity, or *kegare*, and thus should be avoided in a sacred place like the *jinja*.

In some cases, a sacrifice requires giving part of a person's own body. In Lakota traditional religion, various rituals involve cutting the practitioner's flesh as an offering to the *wakan* spirits. In certain Lakota rituals, practitioners may sever small chunks of flesh from their arms, sometimes tying these into a bundle and giving them to the deities as a gift. Better known is the Sun Dance ritual, in which participants skewer their flesh and dance around a sacred pole in the heat of the Plains summer, praying as they do so. In Lakota traditional belief, the suffering endured helps to attract the attention of spirits and makes the prayer more

## PROFILE
HUMAN
SACRIFICE

Understanding human sacrifice is complicated by the fact that it is often recorded by communities other than those allegedly performing it. Accounts of human sacrifice among Germanic peoples – as depicted in this 1882 engraving – come largely from Roman writers, for example. In some places, the archaeological remains of children suggest that they were sacrificed; elsewhere, accounts of criminals being sacrificed suggest blurred lines between human sacrifice and capital punishment.

*AZTEC PRACTICE*
The rulers of the Aztec Empire appear to have sacrificed war captives by dragging them to the top of stone pyramids and cutting out their hearts – a practice that shocked the invading Spanish Christians.

*WICKER MAN*
Roman general Julius Caesar claimed that the Gauls burnt people alive inside a giant wicker man. The practicalities of such a method mean that the accuracy of his claims have been much debated.

*THE WICKER MAN FILM*
Caesar's account has made a long-lasting impact. In the folk horror film *The Wicker Man* (1973), a modern Pagan community on a Scottish island burn a man alive inside a wicker statue to appease the gods.

*LINDOW MAN*
Killed around the 1st century AD, Lindow Man was possibly a human sacrifice. He was placed within a bog in Cheshire, England, from which his well-preserved corpse was revealed in 1984.

*TOLLUND MAN*
Another well-known bog body from northwestern Europe is Tollund Man, found in Jutland, Denmark. He had been killed in the 4th century BC, during the Iron Age, possibly as a human sacrifice.

*GRAUBALLE MAN*
Also found in Jutland, Grauballe Man was killed in the late 3rd century BC. The discovery of numerous Iron Age bodies in the peat suggests a ritual custom that was observed during this period.

**Sacrificial Blades from the Americas**

*Three blades, probably used in sacrificial rituals among Peru's Chimú people, date from the 11th to the 15th century (top). The figure holding a similar blade and a severed head derives from the Peruvian Moche society, which lasted from the 1st to the 8th century (bottom left). Also pictured is a 15th or early 16th-century sacrificial Aztec knife from Mesoamerica (bottom right).*

effective. The flesh is sometimes offered as thanks for a service previously rendered by the spirits.

Human sacrifice appears to have been rare, but it is not unknown. Where it did take place, it may have overlapped with capital punishment. Roman general Julius Caesar (100–44 BC) claimed that the Gauls of Western Europe sacrificed criminals by burning them alive inside a giant wicker man – a scenario that, although perhaps inaccurate, has had a long-lasting impact on perceptions of pre-Christian religion. In the Aztec Empire, slaves and war captives were also sacrificed, in some cases by having their chest cut open with a *tecpatl* flint knife and their beating heart removed. Some societies may have resorted to human sacrifices only in extreme circumstances. Roman historian Livy (59/64 BC–AD 17) noted that, in a time of crisis, the Romans buried four people alive – two Gauls and two Greeks – as a sacrifice at the Forum Boarium. This was, however, against their general custom.

Material objects, sometimes of great craftsmanship and value, are also gifted to deities. These may represent objects that the divinities can use, or they may act as a means of demonstrating the extent of a person's devotion. This can be seen in many parts of Europe during later prehistory and the early Middle Ages, where metalwork (such as swords and spears) was repeatedly cast into lakes, rivers and pools. At Llyn Cerrig Bach, a lake on the Welsh island of Anglesey, for example, Iron Age people cast around 180 metal objects into the water, from shield bosses to parts of a chariot. While we can never be sure of the intentions of prehistoric people, archaeologists typically believe that these represent offerings to the deities. In many cases, the metalwork was deliberately damaged prior to being placed in the water, probably to indicate that this material was no longer to be used by ordinary humans.

★ ★ ★

As modern Pagan religions emerged during the 20th century, they lacked the network of specialized buildings accessible to long-established traditions. To correct this, various modern Pagan groups have

# PROFILE
VOTIVE
OFFERINGS

Much of what is known about the pre-Christian religions of Europe comes from archaeology. Thousands of items have been recovered from across the continent, often in watery contexts such as rivers and wells, which archaeologists believe are votive offerings to the gods. Such offerings were made for thousands of years, although with variations regarding which objects were used and where they were placed. Similar depositions continued into Christian centuries and can be seen in contemporary customs such as throwing coins into a fountain – reflecting the adaptability of human practice to changing ideology.

TRUNDHOLM
SUN CHARIOT
Recovered from a peat bog in Trundholm, Denmark, in 1902, this artefact dates from the Bronze Age. Although made largely from bronze, elements of gold decoration suggest it was a high-status item. Archaeologists have argued that it references a mythological belief in horses pulling the sun through the sky.

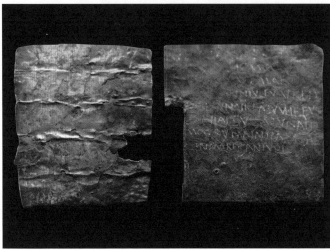

CURSE TABLETS
Around 130 curse tablets have been recovered from the Romano-British temple of the goddess Sulis Minerva in Bath, England, having been put there between the 2nd and 4th centuries. Latin inscriptions on the tablets reveal that people were writing them to invoke the goddess's aid in punishing people.

**BATTERSEA SHIELD**
A decorated piece of sheet bronze that would have fitted over a wooden shield, this object was recovered from the River Thames in London in 1857. Dating from between 350 and 50 BC, during the Iron Age, it represents an example of the La Tène artistic style that was widespread across Europe in this period.

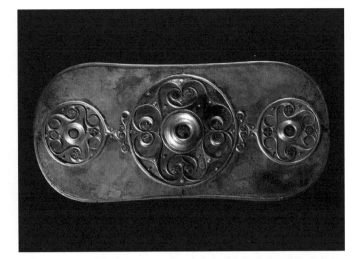

**GUNDESTRUP CAULDRON**
The silver Gundestrup Cauldron was discovered in a Danish peat bog in 1891, having been dissembled into pieces prior to its deposition. Archaeologists date it to between 200 BC and 300 AD, during the Iron Age, although suggest that it was possibly made by Thracians in southeastern Europe before travelling north.

**LLYN CERRIG BACH**
A selection of metal objects were deposited in Llyn Cerrig Bach, a lake on Anglesey, Wales during the Iron Age. These included a plaque (right), weapons including arrowheads (far right), objects of bodily adornment and a chain with manacles that suggest it was used for prisoners or slaves. Many of these objects were deliberately broken prior to being placed in the water.

**Wiccan Solitary Ritual**
*A Wiccan in Rio de Janeiro,
Brazil, performs a solitary ritual.
He inserts the* athame *blade
into the chalice, an act that
conveys sexual symbolism.*

established their own temples, ranging from the Native
Ukrainian National Faith group's building at Spring Glen,
New York, USA, to the Goddess Temple at Glastonbury,
England. These provide spaces for regular worship
by the local community, but also attract pilgrims from
further afield.

Establishing permanent temples is, nevertheless,
not a priority for many modern Pagans. In some cases,
their reasons are practical. In countries such as the
USA, most Pagans are solitary practitioners, and many
groups that do form disband after a short time. Elsewhere,
for example among modern Druids, practitioners may
prefer to conduct outdoor rituals, offering a sense
of being in touch with nature. Various Pagan groups,
especially Wiccans, tend to meet in their members'
homes, which offer greater privacy and make them
less of a target for persecution.

Where modern Pagans have established temples,
they are able to maintain permanent altars or shrines.
For many other practitioners, however, altars are an
ephemeral affair, set up for the duration of a ritual
and then dismantled. The reasons for this may often

**Wiccan Outdoor Ritual**
*Two Wiccans in Rio de Janeiro,*
*Brazil, take part in an outdoor*
*ritual. As is common in Wicca,*
*they perform their ceremony*
*around a fire.*

be pragmatic: the space may be otherwise used for everyday activities or adherents may seek to keep their religious activities a secret from friends, family members or housemates. In some older Wiccan traditions, there is a formal set-up for the altar arrangement, which typically includes candles, a five-pointed pentacle, a censer of incense, a wand and a sword – perhaps accompanied by images or symbols of the Mother Goddess and Horned God. In other forms of Wicca, and in various Pagan religions, the choice of design can be far more eclectic, reflecting the needs and creativity of its creator(s). Alongside images or symbols of deities, material placed upon these altars will often reflect seasonal change, for example by incorporating orange and red flowers and harvested gourds or pumpkins to mark the arrival of autumn.

Also common among modern Pagans, especially in Europe, is the performance of rituals at archaeological sites believed to have been ceremonially important in pre-Christian societies. In Britain, for example, many Wiccan and modern Druid groups perform rituals at the stone circles erected during the Late Neolithic

**PROFILE**
HOME
SHRINES

A common feature of many non-Abrahamic religions is the home shrine, dedicated to family ancestors, major divinities or lesser protective deities, such as the *lares* worshipped by the Romans. Seen here is a 1st- or 2nd-century bronze statuette of a *lar*, which probably once graced a household shrine.

*HINDU SHRINE*
The Hindu home shrine has statues or images (*murtis*) that the deities are believed to inhabit physically. It is here that householders will make their daily offerings and prayers to the gods.

*JAPANESE SHRINE*
Japanese homes may have either a Shinto *kamidana* shrine or a Buddhist *butsudan* shrine (here pictured in Kyoto). The latter is often devoted to a *bodhisattva* or enlightened being who aids others.

*CHINESE SHRINE*
Across the Chinese world, household shrines (here pictured in Malaysia) often contain spirit tablets, thus enabling householders to venerate their deceased ancestors, typically offering incense and paper money.

*SANTERÍA SHRINE*
In the Cuban religion of Santería, initiates may have a household shrine dedicated to their patron *orisha*. These spirits are thought to inhabit small stones (*otanes*), which are housed in porcelain tureens.

*VODOU SHRINE*
There is considerable variation in the home shrines created by Haitian Vodouists. These are devoted to the *lwa* spirits, who may be personified with statuettes sometimes made from recycled objects.

*WICCAN SHRINE*
As most Wiccans practise alone rather than with a group, it is common for them to have household shrines, such as this one featuring images of the Horned God and the Mother Goddess.

and Bronze Ages. Archaeologists do not know exactly what these stone circles were for, with multiple interpretations having been advanced, but it is widely supposed that their function was ceremonial and for this reason they have attracted modern Pagan interest. For modern Pagans, such ancient sites are often also regarded as the dwelling places of ancestral or natural spirits, imbued with certain cosmic forces that can be drawn upon through ritual action.

Although an atypical example, by far the best known of Britain's stone circles is Stonehenge in Wiltshire. Since the 18th century, there has been speculation that it was built by the ancient druids, and while this idea has been dismissed by archaeologists, it has resulted in the circle becoming popular with modern Druids, many of whom perform ceremonies there at the winter and summer solstices. Pagans elsewhere in Europe have also made use of pre-Christian ritual sites. In Greece, for example, modern Hellenes – who revive the worship of the ancient Olympian deities – have ignored bans to perform ceremonies atop the Athenian Acropolis, next to the Parthenon. Pagans have also shown interest in the Neolithic site at Çatalhöyük, Turkey, where excavation has revealed female figurines that are frequently interpreted (correctly or not) as mother goddesses. Members of the Goddess movement, in particular, have been attracted to this site, often perceiving it as evidence of an ancient goddess-worshipping matriarchy.

For today's Pagans, such places are not only valuable ruins from the ancient past, but also fundamentally sacred sites. This has sometimes resulted in conflict with archaeologists and heritage managers, especially when these different interest groups each feel an exclusive sense of ownership over a site. Many heritage managers have expressed concerns that Pagan rituals can damage archaeologically sensitive areas, while some Pagans have opposed archaeological excavations – as at the Seahenge timber circle in Norfolk, England, for example – because it can involve dismantling ancient ceremonial structures.

**Modern Druids
at Stonehenge**

*Various modern Druid groups have performed ceremonies at Stonehenge, on
Salisbury Plain in Wiltshire, England, since the early 20th century. This group, the
Druid Order, were photographed during the 2014 summer solstice. The prehistoric
ceremonial site features a unique stone circle, which was constructed in the late
Neolithic period in c. 2500 BC.*

## DECODING
STONEHENGE

Probably the best-known archaeological site in Britain, Stonehenge was transformed over phases in the Neolithic and Bronze Age periods. Although part of a broader tradition of stone circle construction found across Britain and Ireland, its finished form was fundamentally unique. It probably had a ritual purpose for its prehistoric builders, and in the 20th century it again became a site of religious significance, especially among modern Pagan Druids.

1. Station stone
2. Standing sarsen (without lintel)
3. Standing bluestone (inner horseshoe)
4. Lintel (upon two sarsen stones)
5. Altar stone (hidden under fallen sarsen stone)
6. Fallen bluestone
7. Earthen ditch

# WITCHCRAFT

LUCAN, PHARSALIA, BOOK 6

AT LENGTH THE WITCH
PICKS OUT HER VICTIM WITH
PIERCED THROAT AGAPE FIT
FOR HER PURPOSE. GRIPPED
BY PITILESS HOOK O'ER
ROCKS SHE DRAGS HIM TO
THE MOUNTAIN CAVE.

TRANS. SIR EDWARD RIDLEY

One of the things that Abrahamic societies
have often shared with their non-Abrahamic
counterparts is a fear of individuals capable
of harming others through supernatural means.
Typically called 'witches', such individuals have
regularly been seen as embodiments of evil.
In more recent centuries, counter-cultural groups
in Western countries have sought to reclaim
the identity of the witch, infusing it with positive
meanings, something that can be seen most
clearly in the modern Pagan religion of Wicca.

**F**rom famine, drought and poverty through to injury, sickness and death, people's lives are often beset by tragedies that are difficult to understand. In many societies, people have attributed these misfortunes to supernatural forces, among them wrathful deities, malevolent spirits and human beings who possess an uncanny ability to harm others through non-physical means. Many societies around the globe have their own names for the latter, but it is the English term 'witch' that has gained the most widespread usage.

Witchcraft beliefs vary, with societies each having their own perceptions of who witches are, why they do what they do, and how they do it. Typically, these preternatural malefactors are believed to be an enemy within, dwelling inside a person's own community – a family member or perhaps a neighbour. In some contexts, the malefactors have been thought to hurt people simply through their will or desire, or even unintentionally. In others, witches are believed to perform rituals, often involving material paraphernalia. They might, for example, mix up potions or command a spirit to do their bidding. While some witches are, therefore, deemed completely responsible for their actions, others are thought to have diminished culpability, not wholly in control of what they do.

Many societies believe that witches invert the fundamental norms and values of their community, becoming the personification of all that is evil. Hence, witches are repeatedly imagined as engaging in nudity, incest and cannibalism, all things widely censured as antisocial. Adding to their antinomian nature, witches are also regularly thought to conduct their activities at night, when most people are asleep. This inversion of normality can extend to fairly trivial aspects of life: a traditional belief among the Amba of Uganda, for example, is that witches eat salt to quench their thirst.

Many traditions maintain that being a witch is an innate trait with which certain individuals are born, often inherited from a parent and evidenced by some physical manifestation on or inside the body. The Hewa people of the New Guinea Highlands, for example, believe that witches have within them a small foetus-like

〈 *page 128*
John William Waterhouse,
*Circe Invidiosa*, 1892
*In Homer's* Odyssey, *Circe is a minor goddess who initially hinders but later assists the hero Odysseus. Many of her traits contributed to later European stereotypes about witches.*

**John William Waterhouse, sketch for *The Magic Circle*, 1886**

*Pre-Raphaelite English painter Waterhouse made much use of imagery from mythology and legend in his art. Here, he incorporates various stereotypical features of the witch, such as the wand, cauldron and magic circle drawn in the earth around the central figure. She appears to be a witch or priestess, and in her hand is a crescent-shaped sickle, linking her to the moon.*

*Scenes of Witchcraft: Morning,*1640, Salvator Rosa

*Scenes of Witchcraft: Day,* 1640, Salvator Rosa

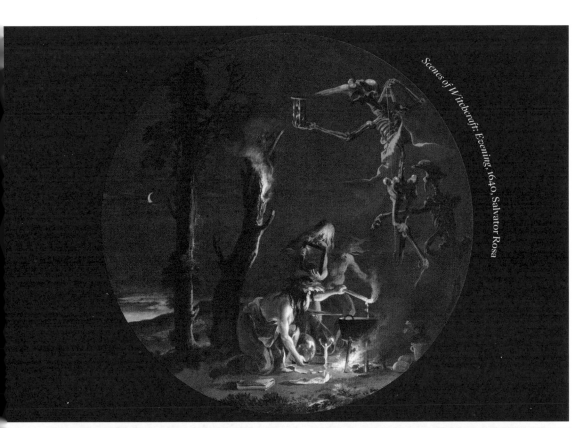

*Scenes of Witchcraft: Evening*, 1640, Salvator Rosa

*Scenes of Witchcraft: Night*, 1640, Salvator Rosa

**Rangda Masks**

*The female demon Rangda is a well-known character from Balinese legend. A traditional dance involves an individual dressing as Rangda and re-enacting her battle with the good spirit Barong. Masks such as those seen here are commonly worn. The elaborate mask at top right was created by Balinese artist I Wayan Murdana at his workshop in Sukawati, Bali, Indonesia.*

entity that compels them to kill in order to satisfy its desire for flesh. Among the Nyakyusa people of Tanzania, a python is thought to dwell inside a witch, and the witch travels on this serpent at night to drain the life from sleeping victims. Some witches are perceived as lone actors, but there is also a recurring notion that witches meet in groups. The Yoruba, for example, traditionally believe in a society of witches, entry into which requires killing one of one's own children.

Contributing to the fantastical nature of these stories is the belief among some that witches have the ability to fly. The traditional view of the Trobriand islanders is that witches flew naked, meeting with one another on reefs out to sea. Supposedly, these witches stole the organs of their human victims to devour at cannibalistic feasts, leaving the unwitting organ donors sick. Other communities believe that witches ride on animals. A traditional Zulu belief is that witches ride backwards upon baboons, while among Shona people it is hyenas that serve as witches' steeds. According to Navajo tradition, meanwhile, the witches themselves transform into animals to feast on corpses. The latter is part of a widespread notion that witches have shapeshifting abilities.

Fantastical witches or similar malevolent beings can become prominent figures in a community's folklore or mythology. As a result, they are depicted in their art. In Bali, for example, the female witch or demon Rangda is portrayed in traditional dances by an individual dressed in a fearsome face mask, with long talons affixed to their fingers.

* * *

Some communities have displayed intense anxiety about witches, but others have regarded witchcraft as a trivial concern. Siberian communities, for example, were traditionally far more prone to blame misfortune on harmful spirits rather than on other humans. A few societies, such as that of the ancient Egyptians, had no concept of the witch at all. Even among societies of believers, bouts of witch-hunting have often come and gone, commonly aggravated by strained economic circumstances or destabilizing socio-cultural change.

Societies that do believe in witchcraft will often have specialists who counteract bewitchment and sometimes identify the witches themselves. To do this, they may employ a range of techniques, often including forms of divination. A practice found among various Central African societies entailed giving poison to the accused witch; if they died, they were deemed guilty. Witch-finders can be figures of power in their society and use their role to their advantage, accusing opponents or political rivals of witchery. Among the Shawnee people of northeast North America, the early 19th-century prophet Tenskwatawa made accusations of witchcraft against members of his people who had converted to Christianity.

Punishments for those deemed guilty of witchcraft have varied. Some societies believed that simply identifying a witch was enough to nullify their power, with little or no further action needed. At the other extreme, accused witches have been executed, sometimes in large numbers. The body of the witch will often be disposed of in a manner different to that of other deceased people. To prevent the dead witch's spirit haunting the living, Greenland Inuit communities, for example, cut up the body into pieces.

\* \* \*

Witches and similar figures appear in the Classical literature of Greece and Rome. Greek legendary epics feature Circe and Medea, both women who use supernatural powers to harm others. However, unlike most witches, this duo are not human; Circe is a goddess and Medea is her niece. They are also not unrelentingly malevolent, for although Circe initially tries to capture the warrior-king Odysseus and turn his men into pigs, she later goes on to assist him. Medea, meanwhile, marries the hero Jason and helps in his endeavours. The way in which these women were portrayed, for example through Circe's use of a wand, nevertheless contributed to later European stereotypes of the witch.

Paulus Bor,
*The Disillusioned Medea,*
c. 1640

*This painting features Medea, a figure from ancient Greek legend who married the hero Jason and later murdered their two sons. Here, Bor portrays her with a wand to highlight her powers as an enchantress. She sits before a pagan altar, decorated with garlands and an ox skull.*

## DECODING
CIRCE

In Homer's epic poem the *Odyssey*, the hero Odysseus encounters the enchantress Circe on the island of Aeaea. Able to transform her enemies into animals, she uses her knowledge of potions to turn his crew into pigs. After the Renaissance, with the revival of interest in the Classical world, Circe became a popular subject for European artists. British Pre-Raphaelite artist John William Waterhouse painted her three times, including here, in *Circe Offering the Cup to Ulysses* (1891).

**CUP**

Circe usually offers her potion to drink from a cup. In *Jealous Circe* (1892), Waterhouse depicts her poised to throw her magic potion into a well where her rival in love, Scylla, is about to bathe.

**WAND**

After administering the potion, Circe taps her enemy with her wand or staff to complete the transformation. She is about to tap Odysseus in Bartholomeus Spranger's painting (*c.* 1580–85).

**ANIMALS**

Circe lures travellers who pass her island of Aeaea to her home and transforms them into docile lions and wolves, as shown in Dosso Dossi's *Circe and Her Lovers in a Landscape* (*c.* 1525).

**BOOK OF SPELLS**

Although Homer did not allude to Circe's spell book in the *Odyssey*, many subsequent artists provided her with one, including Guercino in this 17th-century Baroque painting.

**SCYLLA**

In Ovid's *Metamorphoses*, Circe uses a potion and incantation to transform her rival Scylla into a monstrous sea-beast. Eglon van der Neer captures the moment in this dramatic painting of 1695.

**CAULDRON**

Circe mixes a potion in a cauldron as she waits on the cliff edge, watching for passing sailors to lure to her island, in this Romantic painting of 1910 by Frederick S. Church.

**Early Modern Witches**

*These 18th-century prints reflect the prevalent early modern view that witches were in league with the Devil and assembled to worship him at witches' sabbaths.*

More overtly malicious witches appear in Roman writings, such as the works of Horace (65–8 BC) and Apuleius (*c.* AD 124–*c.* 170), thus suggesting that Roman society had a darker impression of witchcraft than its Greek forebears. In Horace's work, the witch Canidia is a frightening hag who tears apart a lamb with her teeth to collect its blood. She starves a child to death to remove his organs for a love potion and poisons people's food with her own breath. Canidia and other Roman witches used bizarre and rare ingredients in their spells and were associated with nocturnal activity and fantastic feats – one of the witches in Apuleius's work rubbed herself in ointment and proceeded to transform into an owl.

Much of this pre-Christian Classical iconography fed into Christian European perceptions of the witch. The Christian worldview, nevertheless, influenced shifting ideas of witchcraft, especially by associating witches with the Devil. By the early modern period, European Christians widely believed that witches were part of a vast anti-Christian conspiracy. These witches, it was thought, openly worshipped Satan. They assembled to venerate him at nocturnal sabbaths, where they engaged in orgies, desecrated the Eucharist and devoured infants. Fears of this Satanic conspiracy fuelled growing persecution of accused witches across much of Christendom in the 16th and 17th centuries, a period marked by the instability of the Reformation,

T. H. Matteson,
*Examination of a Witch*,
1853
*This painting depicts a scene
from the witch trials that took
place in Salem, Massachusetts,
USA, in 1692-93. The accused
is being inspected for the
marks of a witch.*

Counter-Reformation and widespread warfare. Over the course of this period, around 40,000 to 60,000 people were executed as witches, most of them women and most of them almost certainly innocent.

These trials died down by the 18th century, largely because of growing scepticism among educated sectors of society. Fears about witches as supernatural malefactors, nevertheless, persevered into the early 20th century, albeit without the intense Satanic trappings of the early modern period. These fears largely disappeared only amid modern medical care, social welfare nets and the state suppression of those making witchcraft allegations. In many poorer regions of the world, witch-hunts continue to take place, often with devastating consequences for the accused.

\* \* \*

Although the notion of the 'good witch' would have been totally alien to many past societies, the idea has become increasingly prominent since the 20th century. In large part, this has been due to the appearance of

**Hans Baldung**
*The Witches*, 1510

*In the early modern period, European artistic depictions of witches often emphasized their frightening and anti-social characteristics. This image illustrates many of the stereotypes about witches that were common at this time, including nudity and their ability to fly to the witches' sabbath.*

**Albrecht Dürer,**
*The Witch, c.* 1500

*Dürer's image of a witch as an elderly hag echoes how older women were more commonly accused of witchcraft than any other age or gender group in early modern Europe. Here, the witch rides upon a goat, perhaps alluding to ideas that the Devil took the form of such an animal at the witches' sabbath.*

Evelyn De Morgan,
*The Love Potion*, 1903
*This painting of a woman
mixing a love potion features
a shelf holding several books
about magic, including
the* Third Book of Occult
Philosophy *(1533) by
Heinrich Cornelius Agrippa.*

Marie Spartali Stillman,
*Pharmakeutria (Brewing
the Love Philtre)*, 1870
*In this Pre-Raphaelite painting,
two witches brew a love potion –
an idea that owes something
to Classical figures such
as Circe.*

Wicca: a modern Pagan religion whose followers openly call themselves 'witches'.

Shifting perceptions of witchcraft were facilitated in part by a reassessment of history. During the 19th and early 20th centuries, several scholars suggested that the 16th- and 17th-century witch trials had been an attempt to stamp out a surviving pre-Christian religion. The Devil of the early modern witches, these scholars argued, had actually been an ancient Horned God; those executed had been his worshippers, not just innocent people caught up in the delusions of their persecutors. This notion reached its greatest prominence in the work of British Egyptologist-cum-folklorist Margaret Murray during the 1920s and 1930s, and while it would be conclusively rejected by further historical investigation from the 1960s onward, it had already been absorbed into British intellectual culture.

Publicly emerging in England during the early 1950s, initial adherents claimed that Wicca's origins were in the ancient religion of the Horned God – although they typically maintained that they worshipped a goddess, too. What is more likely is that Wicca was created by occultists who were interested in the work of writers

*A Wiccan priest oversees a handfasting, or wedding ceremony, for two modern Pagans in Canada in 2008. The couple's hands are bound together to symbolize the joining of their lives.*

such as Murray and who used a range of sources to piece together their own new religion. In addition to calling themselves 'witches', the Wiccans met in groups known as 'covens,' conducted rituals that they labelled 'magical' and used tools such as wands and cauldrons, thereby drawing heavily on the visual imagery of magic and witchery as it had long existed in the European cultural imagination.

Rather than hexing and cursing people, these early Wiccans often held to the command that they should 'harm none' when casting spells. Wiccan rituals, therefore, often focused on constructive ends, such as healing or helping people secure employment. Influenced by earlier occultist movements such as Thelema, these Wiccans adopted the idea that concentrated human willpower could bring about real changes in the physical universe – it was this process that they labelled 'magic'. Although often believing that the power of the mind was ultimately all that was needed to work magic, Wiccans typically used ritual tools – most notably the wand and a knife called an *athame* – as a means of concentrating their willpower on their desired purpose.

## PROFILE
THE HORNED
GOD
☿

In the early 20th century, folklorist Margaret Murray argued that many deities who bore antlers or horns actually represented a single divinity – one whom the Christians had interpreted as their Devil. Early Wiccans then adopted Murray's Horned God as a fertility deity. They were influenced by the occultist Eliphas Lévi's 1856 illustration of Baphomet or the 'Sabbatic Goat' (below), which features the head and horns of a beast but the body of a human, and symbolizes the concept of balance.

*THE SORCERER*
During the Upper Palaeolithic period, communities in what is now France painted on the walls of caves. One of these, 'The Sorcerer' in the Cave of the Trois-Frères, Ariège, appears to show an antlered figure.

*CERNUNNOS*
This carving of a head with antlers appears on a Gallo-Roman pillar devoted to the god Jupiter in Paris, France. The accompanying inscription '[C]ernunnos' suggests this was the figure's name.

*THE GUNDESTRUP FIGURE*
An antlered figure adorns this large silver vessel, recovered from a Danish peat bog. Believed to date from the Iron Age, it is not known where the vessel was made, although the Thrace region is likely.

*APOLLO KERAIATES*
A Bronze Age figurine discovered at Enkomi, Cyprus, wears a horned helmet. Although popularly called the 'Apollo Keraiates' or 'Horned Apollo', links with the later god Apollo are probably tenuous.

*BAPHOMET*
One of the accusations made against the medieval Knights Templar was that they worshipped a deity named Baphomet, now thought to be a corruption of the name 'Mahomet' (Muhammad).

*LUCIFER*
Belgian artist Guillaume Geefs' sculpture of Lucifer from the 1840s followed the growing Romanticist tendency to perceive the fallen angel as a rebellious anti-hero with some admirable traits.

Wicca proved popular and spread swiftly to North America and Australia. As it developed, practitioners took Wicca in new directions, for example by combining it with second wave feminism and establishing variants designed for gay and bisexual people. These covens often restricted membership to particular identity groups and altered their theologies and practices accordingly, with many feminist-oriented covens, for example, abandoning any veneration of a Horned God and only worshipping a goddess. Other new Wiccan groups adopted their own particular geographical focus, such as the Welsh-oriented Traditionalist Gwyddoniaid and the Italian-oriented Stregheria, or pursued more radically egalitarian approaches, as with the Reclaiming tradition. A growing number of books explaining how the reader could become Wiccan themselves resulted in a dramatic growth in solitary practitioners from the 1970s onward. Some of these texts were aimed at younger readers, resulting in 'teen witch' trends emerging in the late 1990s and again in the late 2010s, often influenced by portrayals of witches on American film and television. In doing so, Wicca established itself as the world's largest modern Pagan religion, with hundreds of thousands of followers internationally.

Wiccans are not the only ones to reclaim the term 'witch'. From at least the late 1960s, various feminists adopted it as a statement of independent female power. Although some are nonreligious, others are committed to modern Pagan spiritualities. Certain Satanist and Luciferian occultists have also used the word, sometimes calling themselves 'traditional witches' to distinguish themselves from Wiccans, and in the 21st century various practitioners of African diasporic traditions have been more open to adopting the term 'witch' and its Spanish synonym *bruja*. In many ways, these reappropriations of the term 'witch' are much like the modern Pagan reuse of the term 'pagan' itself. In both cases, people are taking a word that has borne negative connotations for centuries and using it to set themselves apart from the Christian-dominated mainstream.

**Modern Cinematic Witches**      *Wicca has influenced the portrayal of witches on film from the late 20th century onward, for example in the supernatural horror* The Craft *(1996, top) and the comedy horror* The Love Witch *(2016, bottom). These movies, in turn, have resulted in more people, including many teenagers, developing an interest in practising Wicca.*

## PROFILE
WICCAN
RITUAL
OBJECTS

The modern Pagan religion of Wicca emphasizes the practice of magic, through which Wiccans seek to bring about changes in the physical universe – either by manipulating etheric cosmic forces or by shifting the psychological outlook of those participating in their ritual. Key to Wiccan views on magic is human willpower, with the will being concentrated via ritual actions involving a selection of tools. Many of these tools have long been part of European stereotypes about magic and witchcraft, going as far back as the Classical era, and thus have been used by ritual magicians for centuries before being adopted into Wicca.

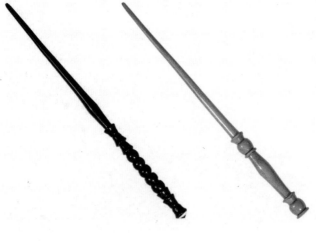

*WAND*
The quintessential witches' tool in European legend, the wand is a long object, often made of wood although sometimes other materials, through which Wiccans seek to direct magical energies. The wand's antiquity is demonstrated by Circe's use of such a tool in Homer's *Odyssey*.

*ATHAME*
The main ritual blade in Wicca, the athame, is not used for physical cutting and certainly not for sacrifice. Instead, it is employed to focus willpower and is sometimes regarded as a symbolic representation of the phallus and of male energies. Some Wiccans use a sword in its place.

## PENTACLE

The pentacle is a material representation of the five-pointed pentagram. For Wiccans, the pentagram is seen as a reference to the five symbolic elements of earth, air, fire, water and spirit. It has also come to be used as a generally recognized symbol of Wicca itself.

## CHALICE

The chalice or cup is often used to hold a drink (typically wine) that is shared among the assembled Wiccans. Symbolically, it is sometimes associated with the vulva and thus female energies, but also with legendary objects such as the Holy Grail and the Cauldron of Inspiration.

## CAULDRON AND BOLINE

Although not found in every Wiccan ritual, the cauldron and boline are used by some Wiccans for practical purposes. The boline is a curved blade used for cutting up herbs for potions. These concoctions are sometimes brewed in a cauldron – an object long associated with witchcraft.

# ORACLES + DIVINATION

NOW I AM AWARE OF NO PEOPLE, HOWEVER REFINED AND LEARNED OR HOWEVER SAVAGE AND IGNORANT, WHICH DOES NOT THINK THAT SIGNS ARE GIVEN OF FUTURE EVENTS, AND THAT CERTAIN PERSONS CAN RECOGNIZE THOSE SIGNS AND FORETELL EVENTS BEFORE THEY OCCUR.

CICERO, ON DIVINATION, BOOK I

TRANS. WILLIAM ARMISTEAD FALCONER

When people are sick, experiencing misfortune or uncertain what to do, they often turn to divination to seek reassurance or guidance. Whether reliant on the casting of yarrow sticks or kola nuts, the reading of tarot cards or direct oracular communication with the supernatural, divinatory practices are generally understood to depend on the wisdom of deities or spirits, entities that can see far beyond the visionary capabilities of human beings.

ivination serves a broad range of functions, from trying to understand the concealed nature of past and present events through to attempts to predict the future. Many people turn to it when they are ill or suffering misfortune and wish to determine both the cause and remedy to their situation. Others employ divination when seeking guidance for making important decisions. In ancient Rome, for example, divination was often employed before people initiated any public business. It was also common for armies to use divination prior to making military decisions. At the Battle of Plataea in 479 BC, the Greek and Persian armies reportedly spent ten days awaiting favourable omens before attacking each other.

Many societies believe that specific divinities are the patrons of diviners. These divinities guide the divinatory process to impart hidden information to the diviner. In Yoruba traditional religion and those American diasporic traditions descended from it, for example, the *orisha* Ọrunmila oversees divination. Surviving prayers from ancient Mesopotamia suggest that the god Šamaš was responsible for divinatory practices there, while among the ancient Greeks it was the god Apollo who bestowed the ability to read signs from the gods. According to one myth, Apollo used his oracle at Delphi to inform the hero Heracles that he had to complete a series of labours for King Eurystheus to secure immortality.

While certain forms of divination can potentially be carried out by anyone, some techniques can only be conducted by trained specialists. Gaining this specialism often requires both initiation and an apprenticeship with a pre-existing diviner, and it can take a considerable amount of time. Among the Yoruba, becoming a *Babalawo* – a diviner skilled in the *Ifá* system – can require ten years of training, after which the 'student' is tested to assess their suitability.

It is often held that an individual destined to become a diviner is impelled to do so by spiritual forces that can induce forms of madness or sickness, ailments that will only be alleviated once the person agrees to train as a diviner. The North Yaka of the Democratic Republic

<page 152
John William Waterhouse,
*The Crystal Ball*, 1902
*Divination using a crystal
ball is a recurring practice
in European societies.*

*Sibylle chez les Romains.*

*Aruspice*
*Chez les Romains.*

*Augure.*

*Grand Pontife Romain.*

**L. Labrousse, 1796**

*These hand-coloured copperplates were drawn and engraved by Labrousse for Jacques Grasset de Saint-Sauveur's* L'antique Rome. *The four ancient Roman ritual specialists are a sibyl (top left), haruspex (top right), the Pontifex Maximus (bottom right) and an augur (bottom left) – several of whom served as diviners.*

**South African Diviner**
*This photograph portrays a man in South Africa divining through the casting of bones.*

of the Congo, for example, believe that a person called on to become a diviner will enter a trance and perform unusual feats, such as jumping onto roofs, rapidly climbing trees or digging holes with their bare hands at a remarkable speed. Once these signs have been understood, the person is expected to train in the art of divination.

Reflecting their role as intermediaries between humanity and spirit forces, diviners will sometimes enter an altered state of consciousness during the divining process itself. In some cases, they believe that a spirit or deity actively possesses them for the duration of the procedure. Diviners among the Batammaliba people of Togo, for example, often describe a feeling of dizziness, akin to being drunk, while they divine. In many communities, diviners also function as healers and may oversee healing practices after diagnosing their client's problem.

★ ★ ★

**African Divination
Material**
*Originating from late 19th
or early 20th-century Africa,
the set of bones, with
accompanying bag (left)
is of unclear provenance,
and the bones carved into
the shape of fish (right) are
from Zambia.*

Many forms of divination involve cleromancy (the casting of lots), after which the diviner draws interpretations from the way in which the objects fall. The *Ifá* system, for example, typically requires casting palm or kola nuts onto a special wooden divining tray. The way in which the nuts fall is then read as a response to the *Babalawo*'s questions, with hundreds of permeations being possible. In China, yarrow sticks are commonly used for divination, and the responses are interpreted through the teachings of an influential divining manual, the *Yijing (I Ching)* or *Book of Changes*, which was first assembled at some point between the 10th and 4th centuries BC.

At a Shinto *jinja* or shrine, it is common to find a box containing sticks. After the box is shaken, one stick will fall out, corresponding to a number that leads the visitor to a specific *omikuji* (slip of paper), on which a prediction is written. If the prediction is bad, the *omikuji* can be tied to a frame or tree in the *jinja*, thereby discarding the bad luck that the *omikuji* itself predicted.

## PROFILE
*YIJING*

The *Yijing*, sometimes transliterated as *I Ching*, is translated as the *Book of Changes*. Outlining a system of divination that interprets hexagrams, the oldest parts of this Chinese text have been attributed to the 12th century BC. Chinese divination systems gained influence across much of East Asia, reflected, for example, in this photograph of a Japanese diviner from the 1910s.

**YARROW STICKS**
The traditional method employed in *Yijing* divination involves casting yarrow sticks, from which a series of hexagrams are deduced. The sticks are made from dried yarrow plant stalks.

**COIN**
In a simple method of divination that emerged over a thousand years after the yarrow stick method, three coins are tossed and the side they land on is used to create a hexagram.

**TURTLE SHELL**
In ancient China, a common divinatory method involved heating turtle shells and interpreting the ensuing cracks. This example of *c.* 1200 BC has been inscribed with annotations.

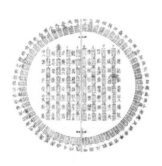

**HEXAGRAM**
Owned by German philosopher Gottfried Leibniz, this early 18th-century diagram has a central grid of hexagrams. Hexagram lines can be broken or solid, representing *yin* and *yang*.

**BOOK OF CHANGES**
This printed copy of the *Yijing* dates from the period of the Song Dynasty (960–1279). In this period, philosophers used the *Yijing* to examine important metaphysical questions.

**DICE**
Dice that have an even number of faces have also been used to carry out *Yijing* divination and are capable of producing the same probabilities as yarrow sticks or coins.

**Congolese Divination Board**

*Dating from the late 19th or early 20th century, this* itombwa, *or friction divination board, is in the style of an animal and was used by a Kuba community in what is now the Democratic Republic of the Congo.*

Among various Central African societies, such as the Zande and the Yaka, rubbing boards are used for divination. These are handheld wooden devices that rub a piccc of wood against another surface, usually another piece of wood or metal, with lubrication sometimes added to assist the process. While rubbing the two surfaces together, the diviner makes statements regarding the problem to be solved. When friction prevents the boards from rubbing anymore, the diviner interprets this as a response to their most recent statement and makes decisions accordingly.

The movement of liquid can also be used for divination. An ancient Egyptian papyrus from 1250 BC describes a technique that involves dropping moringa oil into water and divining from the ensuing patterns. Examining human movement is another type of divination. Among West and Central African societies, such as the Lobi, Senufo and Bena Lulua, a form of divination is practised that anthropologists call 'hand-shaking-muscle-reading'. This involves the diviner and client sitting side by side, holding hands. The diviner then draws meaning from the manner in which the client's arms move in response to the questions.

Animals are sometimes incorporated into divinatory practices. Among some West African societies, diagrams are drawn in the sand and left overnight. The diviner then draws conclusions from how animal tracks have interacted with different areas of their diagram. The type of animal the diviner wants to walk across

Dogon Divination
Drawing
*A Dogon diviner in Mali made
this series of sand markings
for divinatory purposes.*

their drawing varies among communities. Among the Dogon of Mali, for example, it is the pale fox that is favoured, whereas the Kaka Tikar of Cameroon look for the tracks of a ground-dwelling spider. The directions of birds flying in the sky have also been used for divinatory purposes, as with augury practised by the ancient Romans.

Another form of divination entails examining the entrails of a slaughtered animal. Ancient Greeks and Romans often used an animal that had been sacrificed to a deity for this purpose. Once the victim's carcass had been butchered, diviners known to the Romans as *haruspices* would inspect its entrails. A *haruspex* would look at the liver in particular and determine meaning from its appearance. This tradition was reputedly adopted from Mesopotamia. Abnormalities would be read as an indication that the person overseeing the sacrifice might face disaster. Traditionally, the *haruspices* themselves were not from Rome but from Etruria in central Italy. They initially worked independently until Roman Emperor Claudius (10 BC– AD 54) instituted a college of *haruspices* in AD 47.

It is possible that similar forms of divination involved human victims. Writing in the 1st century BC,

Syrian-born Posidonius (135–51 BC) claimed that among the Cimbri – a people living somewhere in continental Europe – priestesses clad in white cut the throats of their prisoners. According to this account, the priestesses poured the blood into a large bronze vessel, divining messages from how it flowed, and then cut out the corpses' entrails to glean further divinatory information. Whether this practice genuinely took place, or is a result of the fantastical and frightening tales people have often told about foreigners, is unclear.

* * *

Not all forms of divination involve material objects or the observation of natural phenomena. Some entail a person seeking direct communication with supernatural entities through mediumship. Among the Māori, such a seer is known as a *matakite*. These people are believed to receive messages from the gods, which they then often present to an audience in the form of a song. In the Nyole communities of Uganda, a seer will shake gourd rattles and sing songs to please the *ehifumu* ancestral spirits, thus allowing one of these entities to possess and speak through them. As the spirit's words are sometimes incomprehensible, the diviner may have to translate for the client.

In ancient Greece, a seer was known as a *mantis*. Ancient Greek literature contains several such characters, including Theoklymenos, who in the *Odyssey* correctly predicts many of the events that take place in the story. The ancient Greeks also held that oracles based at specific sanctuaries could provide insights from the gods. The oldest was reputed to be Dodona, based at the sanctuary of the god Zeus in Epirus. There, diviners allegedly interpreted messages in the rustling leaves of a sacred oak tree. Also popular was the Pythia, an oracle who served at the Temple of Apollo in Delphi. It was originally held that the Pythia received messages from Apollo only once a year, at a spring festival, but as the temple oracle became more popular the Pythia was expected to divine more regularly. To do so she would enter the *adyton*, a sunken area in the centre of the temple, and inhale vapours coming up from a

**Alexandre Cabanel,**
*Velléda*, 1852

*According to the Roman historian Tacitus, Veleda was a prophetess among the Bructeri people of northern Germany who predicted a Bructeri victory in their rebellion against Roman imperial rule in AD 69. Cabanel's Romantic painting includes Gaius Julius Civilis, standing behind Veleda in the shadows, joyous as she predicts his victory.*

## DECODING
THE ORACLE
AT DELPHI

A priestess of the god Apollo, the Pythia served as an oracle, experiencing visions after imbibing vapours rising from the floor of an inner room at the Delphi temple complex – as seen here in *The Oracle* by Camillo Miola (1880). Over time, the Pythia became the most influential oracle in all of Greece, and today the ruins of Delphi are a UNESCO World Heritage Site.

1. Sacred smoke
2. Omphalos
3. Priest of Apollo
4. Pythia
5. Tripod and Bay
6. Supplicant
7. Plinth with inscription describing Apollo's establishment of the temple.

**Arithmancy Manual**
*Written in the Arabic language,
this 19th-century Moroccan
manual explains arithmancy,
or divination using numerals.*

chasm in the floor. Waving a bay branch, she would enter a trance and relay messages believed to come from Apollo himself.

Oracular practices may also have existed in northern Europe. The Icelandic *Saga of Erik the Red*, probably composed in the 13th century, describes the activities of a seer named Thorbjörg. Tasked with predicting the fate of a Norse community in Greenland, she performed an oracular rite during which she sat on a raised platform, surrounded by chanting women, and called the spirits to her. This achieved, she looked into the future, determining that the community's situation would improve. The *Saga* is a work of fiction produced in a Christian context, but it may draw upon knowledge of *seiðr*, a ritual system found among pre-Christian Norse communities.

\* \* \*

Divination is also popular among modern Pagans. Wiccans, for example, often make use of divinatory techniques that evoke magic and witchery in the

**Arithmancy Manual**
*Written in the Arabic language, this 19th-century Moroccan manual explains arithmancy, or divination using numerals.*

**Scrying**
*English Elizabethan astrologer
and magician John Dee (right)
used various objects for
divination, including a crystal
ball (left) and an obsidian
mirror (centre).*

Western imagination. A good example of this is predicting the future using a crystal ball, darkened mirror or bowl of water. Known as scrying, this technique has a lengthy history in European divination. In the 16th century, English esotericist John Dee (1527–1609), for example, used a small crystal ball and obsidian mirror for this purpose. Modern scryers stare into the depths of the crystal, mirror or water, enter a meditative state and then interpret mental images or visions that come to them. Scrying is, therefore, believed to rely on the clairvoyant abilities of the practitioner.

Another example is the tarot, which has been popularly associated with cartomancy (divination using cards) since the 18th century. Tarot cards are typically divided into the Major Arcana and Minor Arcana and they feature images bearing symbolic connotations, such as 'The Magician', 'The Hanged Man' and 'The High Priestess'. Tarot readers randomly select certain cards from the deck and lay them out. Seeking an answer to their own or their client's questions, they draw interpretations from both the symbolism of the cards selected and the order in which they are placed.

The tarot deck probably originated in 15th-century Italy, and for many centuries it was only used for playing card games. As its origins were forgotten, esotericists began to speculate that the images on the cards held secret symbolic meanings, devised in ancient Egypt and transmitted to Europe by the Romany people. Esoteric interpretations of the tarot were further popularized amid the French and British occult revivals

# PROFILE
## TAROT

Tarot cards first appeared in Italy during the 15th century. Originally used as playing cards, they became popular tools for cartomancy, a form of divination. Although not pre-Christian in origin, they are used by some modern Pagans, especially Wiccans, reflecting the influence of older forms of esotericism.

## THE ETTEILLA TAROT

This set of tarot cards was created by French esotericist Jean-Baptiste Alliette in the 18th century. Alliette, who used the pseudonym 'Etteilla' (his name spelled backwards), was a key figure in popularizing the tarot's use for cartomancy.

of the 19th century, before being passed onto Wicca and other 20th-century Pagan movements. Eventually, new versions of the cards catering to Pagan interest were produced, such as the *Tarot of Wicca* (1983) and the *Faery Wicca Tarot* (1999), while other cards for cartomancy, often sold as 'oracle cards', have also drawn on pre-Christian deities and imagery.

Many Pagans prefer forms of divination more closely associated with the pre-Christian world. Among Heathens, whose religion is based on the pre-Christian traditions of Germanic-speaking peoples, runes are often favoured for divination. A linear alphabet used for Germanic languages, runes existed from at least the 2nd century and in some places continued in use right through to the early modern period. While there is no unambiguous evidence that runes were used for divination in pre-Christian periods, ancient Germanic speakers probably did employ divination. Working in the 1st century, the Roman writer Tacitus (*c.* 56–*c.* 120) described how one Germanic group divined using slips of wood. In modern runic divination, the letters are etched onto pebbles, crystals or slips of wood, bone or antler. The diviner asks a question and then either randomly selects several of the rune stones from a bag or casts them all onto a flat surface, observing which fall with their runic letter facing upward. Each letter is associated with a specific meaning, and it is these meanings that are used to answer the diviner's question.

Pagans whose interests lie more in the Celtic-speaking societies often use an alternative alphabetical system to the runes, known as *ogham*. The *ogham* alphabet was used from at least the 4th century in parts of Ireland and Britain, before it – like the runic system – was eclipsed by the Latin alphabet. Modern *ogham* divination operates in a manner similar to runic divination, although the *ogham* letters are typically inscribed onto twigs. Each *ogham* letter is associated with a particular tree species to which its meanings are connected. In this way, both modern runic and *ogham* divination systems have given a new purpose to what are otherwise extinct writing systems.

**Ogham Stone**
    This stone monolith stands in the ruins of Saint Declan's Oratory, Ardmore, County
    Waterford, Ireland. The ogham inscription on the monolith refers to the personal name
    of an individual, thus suggesting it was a memorial. The marks usually read from the
    bottom left-hand side upwards, across the top and then down the other side.

# DECODING
RUNES

Used for the writing of several Germanic languages, the runic alphabet existed by the 2nd century. An early version of the alphabet, now called the Elder Futhark, contained twenty-four letters, although various runes have since been added or removed. Historically, runes were often used to decorate objects, such as the 8th-century Franks casket (below). The suggestion that they originally held a religious purpose has inspired many modern Pagans to use runes primarily for divination.

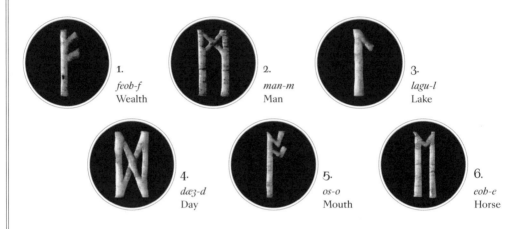

1.
*feoh-f*
Wealth

2.
*man-m*
Man

3.
*lagu-l*
Lake

4.
*dæʒ-d*
Day

5.
*os-o*
Mouth

6.
*eoh-e*
Horse

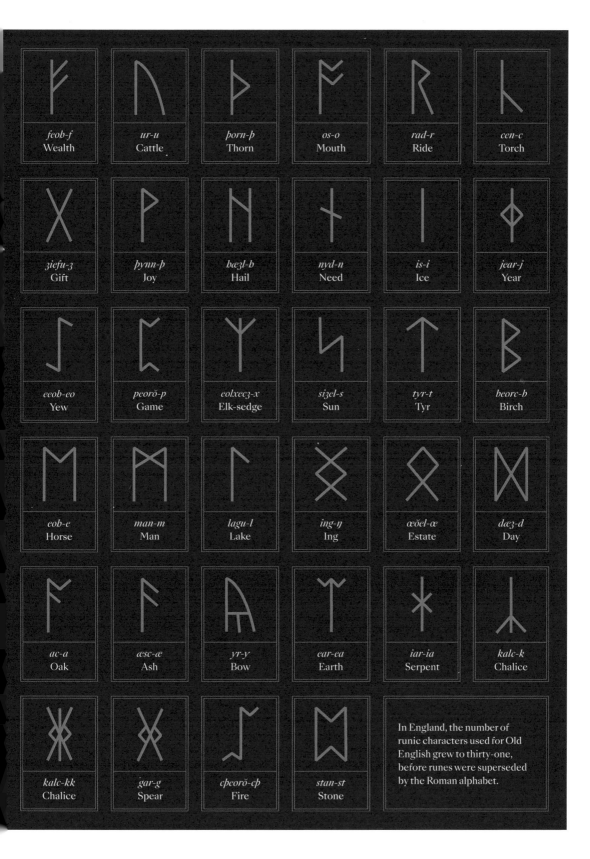

| | | | | | |
|---|---|---|---|---|---|
| *feoh-f*<br>Wealth | *ur-u*<br>Cattle | *þorn-þ*<br>Thorn | *os-o*<br>Mouth | *rad-r*<br>Ride | *cen-c*<br>Torch |
| *ʒiefu-ʒ*<br>Gift | *þynn-þ*<br>Joy | *bæʒl-b*<br>Hail | *nyd-n*<br>Need | *is-i*<br>Ice | *jear-j*<br>Year |
| *eeoh-eo*<br>Yew | *peorŏ-p*<br>Game | *eolxecʒ-x*<br>Elk-sedge | *siʒel-s*<br>Sun | *tyr-t*<br>Tyr | *beorc-b*<br>Birch |
| *eoh-e*<br>Horse | *man-m*<br>Man | *lagu-l*<br>Lake | *ing-ŋ*<br>Ing | *œŏel-œ*<br>Estate | *dæʒ-d*<br>Day |
| *ac-a*<br>Oak | *æsc-æ*<br>Ash | *yr-y*<br>Bow | *ear-ea*<br>Earth | *iar-ia*<br>Serpent | *kalc-k*<br>Chalice |
| *kalc-kk*<br>Chalice | *gar-g*<br>Spear | *cþeorŏ-cþ*<br>Fire | *stan-st*<br>Stone | | |

In England, the number of runic characters used for Old English grew to thirty-one, before runes were superseded by the Roman alphabet.

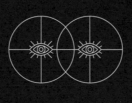

/kə'mjuːnɪti/noun

*The condition of sharing certain attitudes and interests in common.*

# FESTIVALS

SOLMONATH CAN BE
TRANSLATED AS THE MONTH
OF CAKES BECAUSE IT WAS
THEN THAT THEY OFFERED
CAKES TO THEIR GODS.
RHEDMONATH TAKES ITS
NAME FROM A GODDESS
OF THEIRS, RHEDA, WHOM
THEY USED TO SACRIFICE
TO IN THAT MONTH.

Festivals mark a special time apart from everyday life, when ordinary work pauses and people celebrate their ancestors or deities, entities that often appear before them in manifested form. These festivals are regularly held at especially important times in the year for the subsistence of a community, periods at the start of the planting, harvesting, fishing or hunting season, and at which it is vital to cultivate the favour of powerful forces that can ensure success for these vital endeavours.

T he idea that certain times of year are special and should be marked out through ritual and celebration exists around the world. Among non-Abrahamic societies, these festivals often commemorate a specific period in the seasonal or agricultural cycle, or may mark a special point in the relationship between a community and their deities. Festivals create a pause in routine, allowing people to take time out from their everyday labours. They help to bind a community together, cultivating a sense of communal solidarity and inviting people to devote time to visual and artistic displays.

Many festivals are widely celebrated across a large area, forming part of the folk culture of a whole society. Others are more localized, celebrated by a single community and sometimes centred on a local place of worship. This mix of widespread and local festivals can be seen in many places, from ancient Egypt to contemporary Japan. Shinto festivities in Japan, for example, often take place around the same time of year – especially at the new year period of *shogatsu* – even if the manner of celebration reflects regional and localized diversity. There are also unique festivals celebrated in specific towns or villages, typically involving a local *jinja* or shrine.

\* \* \*

Many festivals mark a change in the season, something that is especially important for communities whose existence depends on seasonal food sources. Some festivals celebrate the planting or harvesting of crops, while others highlight points in the year that are crucial for hunting or fishing. Among Coast Salish communities in the Pacific Northwest, for example, great importance is placed on the annual start of salmon fishing, historically a vital part of these societies' subsistence. To celebrate the first salmon caught, community members welcome the fishermen ashore, where the fish is carefully filleted and its flesh consumed. The salmon's skeleton is preserved and ritually returned to the water, accompanied by prayers designed to ensure that the people have a bountiful salmon harvest that year.

‹ *page 175*
**Morris Dancers**
*Historical speculation that Morris dancing may have pre-Christian origins has attracted some modern Pagans to this traditional English folk dance.*

‹ *page 176*
**Man in Tafarron Costume**
*Held the day after Christmas, the festival of San Esteban is popular in parts of Spain. In Pozuelo de Tábara, Zamora, it is celebrated through the Tafarron festival, where traditions include a masquerade featuring the Tafarron, a character pictured here in his straw suit and mask.*

**Japanese *Setsubun***

*Photographed here in 1934, two young women celebrate the Japanese festival of setsubun. Although Japan now follows the European solar calendar, setsubun marks the lunar new year and is usually celebrated on 3rd/4th February. At setsubun, people scatter roasted beans from a wooden box to repel malevolent spirits and invoke good luck for the coming year. This ritual may take place at a Shinto shrine, Buddhist temple or in the home.*

## PROFILE
ZOOMORPHIC
DEITIES

Many societies that believe in a range of gods and goddesses have depicted them in anthropomorphic form, looking more or less like human beings. Sometimes, however, communities have also drawn on other animal species when visualizing their divinities. This can mean either portraying them in wholly animal form or as a composite of human and non-human elements, creating images of the deities that are fully distinguishable from ordinary mortals. This early 16th-century Italian painting by Pinturicchio, from the Palazzo del Magnifico in Siena, Italy, shows three Greek gods, including Pan, a goat-man hybrid.

*GANESH*
In Hindu mythology, Ganesh is the son of the goddess Parvati. When Parvati's husband, Shiva, came home, he did not recognize his son and so beheaded him. Realizing he had to find a replacement head for the boy, Shiva cut off an elephant's head.

*HANUMAN*
This 19th-century painting depicts the popular Hindu deity Hanuman, who is a monkey. He plays a key role in the *Ramayana*, an epic story about Prince Rama, one of the avatars of Vishnu. Devoted to Rama, Hanuman serves as his *vahana*, or vehicle.

*QUETZALCÓATL*
Pictured in this detail of a pre-Columbian Aztec codex, the feathered serpent Quetzalcóatl is associated with death and resurrection. Evidence suggests that the worship of a feathered serpent goes back much further into Mesoamerican history.

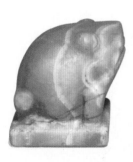

*HEQET*
This statue of *c.* 2950 BC depicts the ancient Egyptian goddess Heqet, who takes the form of a frog. Associated with childbirth and fertility, she is the wife of the god Khnum and, like her ram-headed husband, is connected to the Nile's annual flood.

*KUTKH*
Ravens play a prominent role in the myths of Northeast Asia and the Pacific Northwest. This wooden miniature depicts Kutkh, the creator raven among speakers of the Chukotko-Kamchatkan languages in northeastern Siberia.

*BAST*
This bronze figure (664–630 BC) depicts Bastet or Bast, an ancient Egyptian goddess who takes the form of a lioness or cat. Probably originating from Bubastis in the Nile River delta, her worship later spread across the Mediterranean to Italy.

**Stonehenge Solstice**     *Large numbers of revellers, including many modern Pagans, travel to Stonehenge*
*in Wiltshire, England, to celebrate the rise of the sun on both the summer and winter*
*solstices each year - as pictured here in 2005.*

For agricultural societies, festivals may be regarded as important for ensuring a good crop. In ancient Greece, the festival of Thesmophoria sometimes took place in October, around the time at which crops were sown. Dedicated to the goddess Demeter, it lasted for several days. According to surviving sources, the festival saw pigs being sacrificed and their bodies then placed into subterranean pits called megara. Women subsequently retrieved the rotted remains of previous victims, bringing them up to the surface and placing them upon altars, where the meat was mixed with a seed corn that was then sown into the fields.

Harvest is also an important time for celebration. In West Africa, many societies mark the start of the yam harvest with the New Yam festival, and there is often a general prohibition on anyone eating yams until this has commenced. Among the Fon people who live largely in Benin, the first yams are collected alongside the meat of goats and fowl and offered at the shrines of the deities and ancestors. After the ritual specialists have tasted the yams offered, everyone else may eat.

Some festivals are based on the observation of celestial phenomena. The winter solstice has often attracted attention, marking the point after which the hours of daylight gradually lengthen. This solstice was apparently commemorated by some prehistoric societies in Britain and Ireland, as evidenced by alignments in structures such as Newgrange in Ireland and Stonehenge in England. In the 4th century, midwinter was celebrated by the Romans as the birthday of the sun god Sol Invictus. It has long been argued that this festival influenced the Christian decision to celebrate the birth of Christ in December.

Other festivals are devoted to commemorating the dead. In ancient Rome, the nine-day Parentalia festival in February was intended to honour the ancestors, with people leaving offerings at their family tombs outside the city. In Mexico, *Día de los Muertos*, or Day of the Dead, is ostensibly a Roman Catholic-based holiday, but it may also have indigenous pre-Christian roots. Taking place at the end of October, the festival

**Mexican *Ofrendas***

*To celebrate* El Día de los Muertos, *the Day of the Dead, many Mexicans will create temporary altars called* ofrendas, *dedicated to their deceased loved ones. The* ofrenda *pictured here is dedicated to the artist Rufino Tamayo and his wife Olga and is one of the* ofrendas *displayed in Mexico City's Museo de El Carmen for* El Día de los Muertos *each year. The festival is ostensibly a Roman Catholic one, reflecting the fact that the majority of Mexicans identify as Roman Catholics. It is for that reason, for instance,*

that the pictured ofrenda features a crucifix. Despite the festival's very clear Christian elements, it has often been suggested that El Día de los Muertos was influenced not only by the Catholicism of the Spanish colonialists but also by the pre-Christian religions of Mexico's indigenous peoples. Indeed, as Mexican Catholics have increasingly spread north into the United States, entering areas where Protestants have historically dominated, the latter have sometimes condemned the festival as being pagan.

**The Barque of Amun Arriving at the West Bank of Thebes**
This image is a reproduction of a 13th-century BC depiction of the Beautiful Festival of the Valley, during which statues of the gods Amun, Mut and Khonsu were paraded from their Karnak temple.

is probably the world's best-known celebration of the dead today. *Día de los Muertos* sees Mexicans visit the graves of deceased relatives and build *ofrendas* in their homes, altars at which flowers, candles and food are offered to lost loved ones.

★ ★ ★

A recurring feature in the festivals of many polytheistic religions is a public procession or parade, during which the image of a deity is taken from its shrine and carried around the local area before being returned to its normal abode. By allowing the wider population to see the image, such processions can cultivate a greater sense of communal involvement in religious life. A record from *c.* 670 BC recounts how a statue of the god Bêl or Marduk was clothed and taken out of its temple as part of a procession through the streets of Babylon in Mesopotamia. In ancient Egypt, a parade in which the deity image was removed from its temple was called a *kha* (appearance), a reference to the appearance of the image before the people. Rather than simply parading through the city streets, these processions often took place on the River Nile and for this reason were termed *khenet* (sailings). Reflecting this emphasis on riverine

**Classical Festivals**
*Here, two friezes depict participants in festive processions. One dates from c. 440 BC and is part of the Parthenon frieze, Athens (left); the other, dating from c. AD 100, is found at the Villa of the Quintilii along the Appian Way, Italy (right).*

transport, the sacred images would often be placed in portable palanquin shrines designed to resemble boats.

Although the ancient Greek festival procession, or *pompe*, sometimes involved carrying the deity image through the streets, more usually the images remained within the temple and offerings were brought to them. An insight into such a procession can be seen in the Parthenon frieze, carved in the 5th century BC, which once decorated the temple of Athena atop the Acropolis in Athens. That city saw the Panathenaic procession at the start of the new year, when Athenians paraded through the streets and up to the Acropolis to present their goddess with a new robe, or *peplos*. This act unified the city's residents around their patron deity. Under the name *pompa*, festival processions also took place among the Romans, marking both religious and state occasions. Additional Roman processions were held after a military victory, during which the successful general would enter Rome dressed as Jupiter, king of the gods.

Something of the grandeur of these ancient processions can probably be seen at the festivals that still take place in Indian cities. Among the best known is the annual Ratha Yatra festival in Puri, eastern India, devoted to the god Jagannath, which takes place over seven days in June or July. The image of Jagannath is put into a huge chariot and paraded through the city, accompanied by *sadhus*, or holy men. Those who look upon the image as it proceeds experience *darsan*, a sight of the divinity thought to imbue spiritual merit.

| MENSIS | MENSIS | MENSIS |
| OCTOBER | NOVEMBER | DECEMB |
| DIES·XXXI | DIES·XXX | DIES·XXXI |
| NONAE | NON·QVINT | NON·QVINT |
| SEPTIMAN | DIES·HOR·VIIIS | DIES·HOR·VIIII |
| DIES | NOX·ITOR·XIIIS | NOX·HOR·XV |
| HOR·X·S | SOL | SOL·SAGITT |
| NOX | SCORPIONE | TVTEL·VESTÆ |
| HOR·XIIIS | TVTELA | HIEMPS·NITIV |
| SOL | DEANAE | SIVE·TROPAE |
| LIBRA | SEMENTES | CHIMERIN |
| TVTELA | TRITICARIAI | VINEAS·STERC |
| MARTIS | ET·HORDIAR | FABA·SERENES |
| VINDEMIAE | SCROBATIO | MATERIAS |
| SACRVM | ARBORVM | DEICIENTES |
| | IOVIS | OLIVA·LEGENT |

## DECODING
FESTIVALS OF
ANCIENT ROME

Various festivals were held in ancient Rome over the course of the year, each typically honouring a particular deity. Following the Christianization of the Roman Empire, the dates and customs of some of these pre-Christian festivals may have been absorbed into the emergent Christian calendar of celebration.

### SATURNALIA
Honouring the god Saturn, Saturnalia was held in the middle of December. Festivities were riotous, as depicted here in Antoine-François Callet's *Winter or The Saturnalia* (1783).

### LUPERCALIA
Andrea Camassei's *Lupercalia* (*c.* 1635) portrays the February festival of Lupercalia. During the celebrations, women were whipped as it was believed to make them more fertile.

### CEREALIA
*Spring* (1894) by Lawrence Alma-Tadema depicts a procession of women and girls and may illustrate Cerealia, an April festival devoted to the grain goddess Ceres that involved games in her honour.

### VENERALIA
Peter Paul Rubens depicts Veneralia in *The Feast of Venus* (1636–37). This April festival was held in honour of two goddesses, Venus and Fortuna, and involved ritually bathing statues of Venus.

### FLORALIA
Giovanni Battista Piranesi's *The Empire of Flora* (*c.* 1743) portrays Floralia, an April celebration of Flora, the goddess associated with spring, vegetation and flowers, shown here in her hair.

### VESTALIA
In *The Vestals* (1666), Ciro Ferri paints the priestesses of Vesta maintaining their sacred fire. Vesta is the goddess of the hearth and is celebrated with the June festival of Vestalia.

**Durga Puja**
*A statue of the goddess Durga is immersed in water at the Durga Puja festival in Mumbai, India.*

In addition to being a festival for the people of Puri, the procession also attracts pilgrims from further afield. Similar celebrations are held elsewhere in India. In West Bengal, for example, the Navaratri festival, which takes place each autumn and is devoted to the female divine, often ends with large sculptures of goddesses such as Durga being paraded to the river and then permanently submerged beneath the waters.

Festival processions also remain an important part of Shinto, where they are called *gyōretsu*. Here, the *kami* enshrined at a *jinja* is placed inside an ornate *mikoshi* (palanquin) and carried around the local area. Young men typically carry the *mikoshi*, having been ritually purified beforehand. Often, the *kami* is taken down to the beach and sometimes immersed in the sea itself. At other times, it is taken to a temporary shrine for a short period or on a visit to the permanent shrine of another *kami*. Processions in which images of the deity are carried through the streets are also found in many Roman Catholic societies, where it is usually the Virgin Mary who is treated in this fashion. This practice is anathema to many Protestants, who insist that it constitutes pagan idolatry. Indeed, it demonstrates

Utagawa Hiroshige,
*Brocade Parade of the
Eastern Capital: A View
of Hachiman Shrine at
Ichigaya*, 1860
*This woodcut print features
a Japanese gyōretsu festival
procession, with women
carrying a sedan chair from the
Hachiman Shrine at Ichigaya.*

the way in which many Christian rituals bear strong
similarities to those of non-Christian communities.

\* \* \*

Modern Pagan groups have adopted their own calendar
of festivals, typically drawing upon the celebrations
of historical, and often pre-Christian, communities.
When Wicca emerged, its practitioners adopted four
festivals each year: Samhain or Halloween (31 October),
Imbolc or Candlemas (2 February), Beltane or May Eve
(30 April/1 May), and Lughnasadh or Lammas (1 August).
These are all festivals that have been celebrated by
various historic communities in Ireland and Britain,
in some cases having pre-Christian forms but later
taking on Christian symbolism. The Wiccans termed
each of these festivals 'Sabbats', in reference to the
'witches' sabbaths' that early modern witch-hunters
alleged took place at night. At Sabbats, Wiccans focus
on celebration, rather than the ritual spell casting that
takes place at other meetings.

## PROFILE
THE WHEEL
OF THE YEAR

Modern Pagan religions typically place great interest in the seasonal festivals of past societies, especially those that can be traced back to pre-Christian periods. In the 1950s, English Wiccans established a system of eight annual festivals that came to be embraced by other Pagan groups under the name 'Wheel of the Year'. Individually, many of these festivals were celebrated by earlier societies in Britain and Ireland, although they never existed as an eightfold set until the middle of the 20th century.

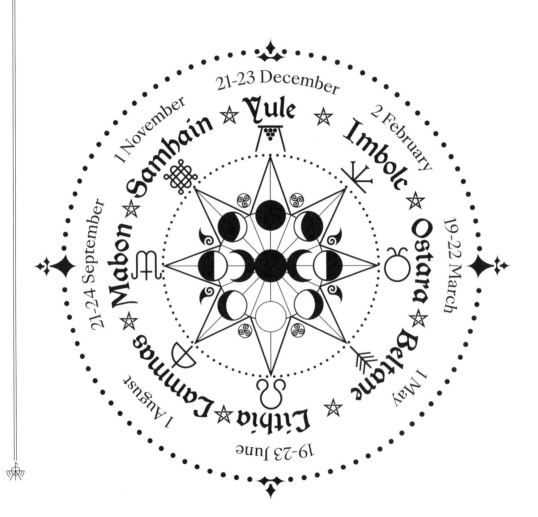

*YULE*
Yule or Midwinter marks the winter solstice, the shortest day and longest night of the year. Some Yule customs, like the Yule log, have been reimagined as Christmas traditions.

*IMBOLC*
Imbolc observes the first stirring of spring in Britain. The festival was originally associated with Brigid, the pre-Christian Irish goddess of wisdom, blacksmiths, poetry, healing and childbirth.

*OSTARA*
Taking its name from a Germanic goddess, Ostara celebrates the spring equinox. Bede describes the festival in *The Reckoning of Time*, though by his time it had been replaced by Paschal month.

*BELTANE*
Equating largely with May Day, Beltane marks a period of long-standing celebration in Britain. One tradition involves driving cattle between two bonfires to protect them from disease.

*LITHA*
Litha or Midsummer is the summer solstice, the longest day and shortest night of the year. The day is celebrated by cultures around the world and customs often centre on nature.

*LUGHNASADH*
Lughnasadh celebrates the start of the harvest, often marked by the symbolic sacrifice of the crop. In Irish myth, the festival is said to have been started by the god Ludh as a tribute to his mother Tailtiu.

**Celebrations of Samhain**    *Modern Pagans have played a key role in reviving Samhain, a celebration historically observed in Ireland, the Isle of Man and Scotland. They are seen here in Edinburgh, Scotland (top), and Vittorio Veneto, Italy (bottom).*

In 1958, Wiccans who were part of the early Bricket Wood coven based in Hertfordshire, England, additionally adopted the quarter days – comprising both solstices and both equinoxes – as 'lesser Sabbats'. They included the winter solstice, commonly termed Yule, the spring equinox often called Ostara, the summer solstice referred to as Litha and the autumn equinox or Mabon. Thus arose an eightfold system of religious festivals, which soon became known as the 'Wheel of the Year'. Although the individual festivals themselves had often been observed by pre-Christian communities, the idea of these eight as a set was wholly new. This festival calendar has also been adopted by Druids and other members of the modern Pagan milieu. For many Pagans, having these celebrations at different points in the year encourages them to observe and enjoy the changing seasons. It also reinforces the feeling that they are following a 'nature religion' in tune with the rhythms of Earth.

Other modern Pagan groups have their own festivals. Many Heathens, for example, celebrate festivals that they believe were originally marked by the pre-Christian societies of Germanic-speaking Europe and that are referenced in historical sources such as the Old Norse *Heimskringla* (*c*. 1220), written by Icelandic poet-chieftain Snorri Sturluson (1179–1241). These include some festivals, for example the midwinter celebration of Yule, that are shared with Wiccans, and others such as *Sigrblót* in April and the *Vetrnætr* or Winter Nights in October, which are specifically Heathen. Taking a similar approach are the Rodnovers, who base their new religions on the pre-Christian traditions of Slavic-speaking peoples. Among their key festivals are the midsummer and midwinter celebrations, known among Russian Rodnovers as *Kupala* and *Koročun*, respectively. These modern Pagan festivals often feature practitioners getting together to build a bonfire, assemble a feast and give offerings to their gods.

As modern Pagans remain religious minorities, their festivals are usually private group affairs rather than events that bring them together with their neighbours.

## PROFILE
## THE GREEN MAN

In the 11th century, European stonemasons began adding carved foliate heads to the decoration of churches, an image that early 20th-century scholars suggest had secretly represented a surviving pre-Christian god. Although few scholars now subscribe to this idea, it gave birth to the notion of the Green Man, a figure portrayed in various public parks and who many Pagans have adopted as a god.

*ROMAN MOSAIC*
Foliate heads started to appear
as decorative motifs during the
Roman Empire. This example is
from an early Byzantine mosaic
in Constantinople (modern-day
Istanbul, Turkey).

*FOLIATE HEAD*
This elaborate 14th or early
15th-century foliate head is
one of several on the ceiling
of the cloisters at Norwich
Cathedral, Norfolk, England.

*THE GREEN KNIGHT*
This illustration of the Green
Knight is from the single
surviving manuscript (*c.* 1400)
of the English chivalric romance
subsequently titled *Sir Gawain
and the Green Knight*.

*BELLARMINE JUG*
Noted for featuring a bearded
human face, stoneware
Bellarmine (or Bartmann) jugs
were produced in Europe, during
the 16th and 17th centuries.
This example is a witch bottle,
sealed with its contents.

*VERTUMNUS*
Italian artist Giuseppe
Arcimboldo painted human
heads composed of vegetables,
fruits, plants and sea creatures.
This *c.* 1590–91 portrait of Rudolf
II, Holy Roman Emperor, is titled
*Vertumnus*, after the Roman god.

*JACK IN THE GREEN*
A conical or pyramidal
framework covered in foliage
and worn on the upper half of
the body, the Jack in the Green
is part of the English May Day
processions, first recorded
in the 18th century.

**La Maya Festival**

*Held each May, the La Maya festival takes place in the town of Colmenar Viejo near Madrid, Spain. Celebrating spring, it features a girl being declared the 'Maya,' dressed in a traditional outfit and seated among a display of flowers. Across Europe, there*

has been speculation that many folk customs have pre-Christian origins. While this may be the case in some instances, the notion has sometimes been contradicted by in-depth historical research.

However, Pagans have also played a prominent role in larger folk celebrations that unite a varied selection of people, such as the English May Day festival. A long-standing element of English culture, May Day has been celebrated historically with dances around a maypole and parades featuring a large conical framework covered in foliage, known as the Jack in the Green. Such customs have often been thought, sometimes mistakenly, to have pre-Christian roots. Since the 1970s, there have been growing attempts to revive these traditions in various parts of England, with particularly popular local celebrations taking place in towns such as Rochester, Kent, and Hastings, East Sussex. While most of those taking part see May Day as a folk celebration without a religious function, many modern Pagans perceive spiritual significance in this celebration of springtime. It is common to find that many of those involved in organizing and celebrating these festivals are modern Pagans, even if they carry out these roles alongside others who do not share their religious belief and identity.

Pagans in the USA have drawn on elements of European folk culture for their own celebrations. Some American Pagans have created hobby horses for their Beltane festivities, often modelled on a specific example, called the 'obby 'oss, that appears at the annual May Day celebrations in the Cornish town of Padstow. This tradition is regularly claimed (with little supporting evidence) to be largely pre-Christian in origin. Another European folk tradition embraced by a number of American Pagans is the Krampus, a fearsome horned monster traditionally associated with the Christmas period in Alpine communities. Krampus gained popularity in Anglophone Western countries during the opening decades of the 21st century, spawning the establishment of North American *Krampuslauf* processions imitating those found in Alpine Europe. In Philadelphia, Pennsylvania, various Heathens have involved themselves in these new *Krampuslauf*, while in Los Angeles, California, Wiccans have also incorporated Krampus into their Yule celebrations.

**The Burry Man**    *In an annual ceremony that was first recorded in 1687 but is thought to be a much older tradition, the Burry Man is dressed in burrs and paraded on a seven-mile route around South Queensferry, Edinburgh.*

**Crowning the New May Queen**

*The new six-year-old May Queen passes through a guard of honour on her way to the crowning ceremony in Staines, Surrey, England, 1934.*

**Old and New**
**May Queens**

*The new and the retiring May Queens lead the procession together. The children supplied their own dresses and Maypole braids.*

# 2

# ℰMBODIED FAITH

ALSO THE PRIEST HATH UPON
HIS HEAD A THING OF WHITE
LIKE A GARLANDE, AND HIS
FACE IS COVERED WITH A
PIECE OF A SHIRT OF MAILE,
WITH MANIE SMALL RIBBES,
AND TEETH OF FISHES, AND
WILDE BEASTES HANGING
ON THE SAME MAILE.

RICHARD JOHNSON, IN RICHARD HAKLUYT, *THE PRINCIPAL NAVIGATIONS,*

*VOYAGES, TRAFFIQUES AND DISCOVERIES OF THE ENGLISH NATION*

Bodily adornment has long been used
for religious expression, whether that be to
display membership of a particular community,
to provide amuletic protection or to highlight
a person's role as a ritual specialist. Clothing
and other bodywear can also serve a specific
function in ritual contexts, demarcating
the sacred from the profane or helping the
ritualists who wear it to enter an altered
state of consciousness and communicate
with the spirit world.

**H**any societies have adorned the body in a manner inspired by their religious beliefs. The reasons for doing so are varied, from wearing an amulet to invoke supernatural protection to wearing clothing to mark out a person as a ritual specialist.

In ancient Rome, some priesthoods had strict rules regarding their clothing. Rome's *flamen Dialis*, or priest of Jupiter, for example, was forbidden from wearing clothes that included a knot, and when outside he was required to wear a special pointed cap called an *apex*. Being a priest was typically not a full-time occupation in Roman society, nor in ancient Egypt. Egyptian records indicate that many temples operated a rota system, with eligible individuals taking on a priestly role for a month at a time. Egyptians serving as priests would typically shave their heads, an act thought appropriate for those operating in a sacred space. Today, a shaven head is also worn by priests in several Hindu traditions, most famously those in the International Society for Krishna Consciousness, founded in 1966. These priests remove most of their hair, except for a lock at the back called a *sikha*, to symbolize their rejection of vanity. For other Hindus, the refusal to cut their hair serves a similar function. Many Hindu *sadhus* let their hair grow and become matted and tangled, thus demonstrating their rejection of normal worldly life in favour of spiritual pursuits.

Ritual specialists often wear clothing that departs from the gender norms of their community. Among the Batammaliba people of Togo and Benin, for example, many female diviners wear shorts, clothing that is normally reserved for men. The Chukchi people of Northeast Asia traditionally had ritual specialists called *yirka-laul* (soft men) who, according to Chukchi beliefs, were commanded by spirits to live and dress as women. Sometimes, they took men as husbands – a custom with parallels among several indigenous communities in the Americas. Something similar may have once existed in Europe. The Roman writer Tacitus claimed that a male priest of the Naharvali people wore female clothing, while medieval accounts suggest that the behaviour of the *seiðmenn* (male practitioners of a ritual

< *page 204*
**Book of Dreams**, *c*. 1720
This illustration from a Book of Dreams depicts a Hindu ascetic or sadhu in meditation.

***The Harpist's Stele,***
***1069–945*** BC

*Produced in Egypt during the Third Intermediate Period,* The Harpist's Stele *depicts the shaven-headed harpist Djedkhonsouioufankh performing in worship of the god Ra-Horakhty before a table of offerings. Often portrayed in falcon-headed form, as here, this god is a merger of the sun god Ra and the sky god Horus.*

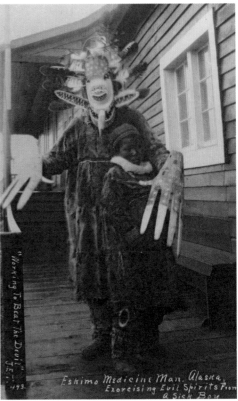

Northern Ritual
Specialists
*These photographs were
taken in the 1890s. On the
left is an indigenous ritual
specialist from a Tungusic-
speaking community in
northern Siberia; on the
right is an indigenous ritual
specialist and a boy he is
treating in Nushagak, Alaska.*

system termed *seiðr*) was deemed at odds with the
masculine norms of Iron Age Scandinavia.

Items of clothing or bodily adornment are sometimes
only worn for the duration of a ritual, helping the ritualist
to get into the required mental space needed to complete
their task. Across central Siberia, it was common for
ritual specialists to put on a highly decorated gown,
accompanied by a headpiece bedecked in feathers
or fur, before performing ceremonies in which they
typically entered a visionary state to heal their patient.
Masks can also be an aid in this regard. Among the
indigenous communities of the Pacific Northwest,
individuals believing that they have received a spirit
power may carve its image onto a mask, which they
then wear at important winter festivals.

Masks are also common in much of Sub-Saharan
Africa, where they are often used to personify
spirits or deities during ceremonies. At the Yoruba

**Yoruba *Egungun***
*Participants representing spirits of the deceased take part in the Egungun festival at Ouidah, Benin, in 2012.*

people's *Egungun* festival, some individuals wear fabric outfits covering both their face and body to personify the *egungun*, or spirits of the dead. The process is sometimes said to induce an altered state of consciousness in the wearer. Among those African diasporic traditions in the Americas – such as Cuban Santería and Haitian Vodou – that derive from the pre-Abrahamic religions of the Yoruba and other West African peoples, clothing is again employed to indicate possession. These religions involve communal rituals in which drumming and singing are used to invoke an *orisha* or (in Haiti) a *lwa*, to possess one of the dancers. Helping to ensure that the individual fully embodies that entity for the duration of their possession, they are dressed in clothing appropriate to the spirit inside them. When a dancer is possessed by the *lwa* Baron Samedi, for example, they may be dressed in a black coat, top hat and dark glasses.

## PROFILE
RITUAL
SPECIALISTS

Many societies have ritual specialists, individuals who have knowledge not accessible to most people around them. These individuals will often play important social roles in their community, whether that be as a diviner, a healer or an intercessor between humanity and their divinities. This Indian image depicts a group of specialists in the Hindu practice of yoga.

*KANNUSHI*
This photograph (1900–06) by H. G. Ponting is of a *kannushi*, a Shinto priest who oversees offerings to the *kami* enshrined at particular *jinja*. They also conduct rituals such as weddings or blessings.

*HATÁÁ£II*
Among the Navajo people, the *hatáá£ii* are the ritual specialists responsible for healing rituals. They learn lengthy songs for this specific purpose. One Navajo *hatáá£ii* is pictured here in *c.* 1914.

*SANGOMA*
Among the Zulu of Southern Africa, the *sangoma* diagnoses problems, and then appeases the ancestors responsible or provides herbal remedies. This photograph of a *sangoma* dates from 1901.

*MAPUCHE MACHI*
The Mapuche of Argentina have ritual specialists called *machi*, whose connections with the spirits enable them to dispel harmful supernatural entities and heal the sick.

*MUDANG*
The *mudang* of Korea are ritual specialists tasked with communicating with the spirits via the *kut* ritual. In doing so, they identify the cause of and cure for misfortunes.

*WICCAN HIGH PRIESTESS*
Each Wiccan coven is usually led by a high priestess, sometimes accompanied by a high priest. This priestess will often call on the Goddess to enter her during a ritual.

## Classical Amulets

*The bronze winged phallus (left) is of Greco-Roman origin. The gold Etruscan bulla (right), dating from the 5th century BC, features the mythological figures of Daedalus and his son Icarus.*

★ ★ ★

Many societies have held to a belief in amulets: physical objects worn on the body that are regarded as having some form of supernatural power. The purpose of these amulets varies, but they are most commonly intended to ensure the protection of the wearer. In ancient Roman society, amulets taking the form of phalluses were associated with the deity Fascinus. They were thought to help protect children and were hung around the necks of babies to prevent them being harmed by the evil eye. The locket-shaped *bulla* was worn by male children to repel harm. When a youth reached the age of manhood, he would dedicate his *bulla* at the domestic shrine of the *lares*, the deities entrusted with protecting the family.

Many non-Abrahamic societies active today make widespread use of amulets. Small shops commonly found at Japan's Shinto shrines supply amulets called *omamori*, each of which is devoted to a specific purpose, such as assisting the wearer in an exam or protecting them from traffic accidents. Shinto's adherents often buy these *omamori* at New Year, believing that they retain their power for the next twelve months. After a year, adherents return

*The tyet symbol (left) dates from the 1st millennium BC and is associated with the goddess Isis. The Wedjat eye of Horus (right) dates from the 4th century BC.*

to the shrine to burn their amulets and purchase replacements.

Many societies have placed amulets in the graves of the dead. Ancient Egyptian amulets were most commonly found in the graves of infants and young women, suggesting that the Egyptians saw these groups as being especially vulnerable and in need of amuletic protection. From 1350 BC onward, the Egyptians made increasing use of amulets in the form of the *tyet* symbol, which appears to be associated primarily with women and Isis, a goddess associated with healing.

In some instances, it is possible that an object worn on the body might have had other uses. Between the 9th and 11th centuries AD, people in Norse communities began wearing pendants in the shape of Mjölnir, the hammer of the god Thor. In Old Norse mythology, the dwarfs Sindri and Brokkr created this hammer, which Thor later wielded in his battles against the enemies of the gods. It is likely, therefore, that those wearing these pendants were seeking to invoke Thor's protection. It is also notable, however, that these pendants came into use at the same time as Christianity was spreading into Scandinavia. In this context, wearing a pendant of

## PROFILE
AMULETS

Whether they are worn on the body, fixed to the wall at home or in the workplace, or even hung from a car's rear-view mirror, amulets are objects believed to wield spiritual forces to benefit the owner. Common functions include attracting good fortune, protecting the owner from harm and repelling witchcraft, bad spirits and the evil eye. Although many Christians have employed amulets in their daily lives, some regard their use as an intrinsically pagan practice that encourages people to place faith in an object rather than in God.

*BODY PARTS*
Amulets taking the form of a human body part are often carried or displayed in the hope of healing a particular part of a person's anatomy or invoking protective symbolism.

〈 Horned Hand,
   *c.* 1870, Corsica
〉 Limb,
   *c.* 1850, Algeria

*SKELETONS*
Representations of skulls, skeletons and coffins have long been favoured as amulets. Perceived to have supernatural powers, they also act as memento mori, encouraging people to remember their own morality.

〈 Hangman Locket,
   1899, France
〉 Death's Head,
   *c.* 1890, Naples

## ANIMALS

Many animal species are perceived to have traits and abilities helpful to humankind. In Europe, an amulet in the shape of a pig is thought to bring good luck; in Bolivia, a llama amulet is believed to protect a herd.

⟨ Stone Llama,
  1903, Bolivia
⟩ Lucky Pig,
  1890, Europe

## STONES

Precious and semi-precious stones are believed by many to contain special powers. For example, lapis lazuli is said to engender harmony in friendships, moonstone to promote clarity of thought.

⟨ Magatama,
  c. 1860, Japan
⟩ Snake Stone,
  1875, France

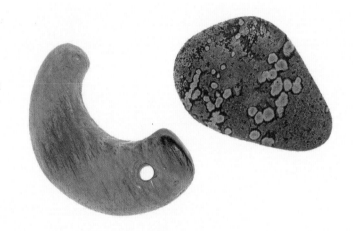

## POUCHES OF PAPER

Scraps of paper, perhaps displaying sacred texts from the Bible or Quran, have been carried in pouches for protection since the Middle Ages. In Islamic cultures, such papers might wrap a medicinal substance.

⟨ Quranic Pouch,
  c. 1900, Algeria
⟩ Textual Pouch,
  1883, France

Charles Hamilton Smith,
*Druids*, 1815
*Smith created these
imaginative reconstructions
of the Iron Age druids for a
book published in 1815. The
images are titled* Costume
of the Druidicial Order *(left)
and* An Arch Druid in his
Judicial Habit *(right).*

Mjölnir could be a statement of religious identity in
the face of an incoming belief system, a counterpart
to the Christian wearing of the cross.

\* \* \*

Choices of physical appearance play an important
role in modern Pagan ritual. One of the distinguishing
features of the early Wiccans, for example, was their
tendency to perform their rituals 'skyclad', or naked.
This derived from the long-standing tradition of nude
witches appearing in European art, and also from a
keen interest in naturism on the part of Gerald Gardner
(1884–1964), the 'Father of Wicca', who helped establish
several of the earliest covens. Proponents of ritual
nudity as a contemporary religious practice have
argued that clothing can impede magical energies
flowing from the body. They believe that being naked
emphasizes the equality of all the Wiccans in the coven,
with none of the differentiation in socio-economic
status that clothing can denote.

Today, only a minority of Wiccans embrace ritual
nudity. Many covens favour the wearing of robes,
usually darkly coloured, for their rituals. When working

outdoors, such clothing is more practical, offering warmth and preventing potential arrest for public indecency. Wearing robes is also common among modern Pagan Druids. In this tradition, white robes have long been popular due to their association with the Iron Age druids, a connection that goes back to the writings of Pliny (AD 23–79) in the 1st century. More recent decades have seen other modern Pagan Druids favour robes of more earthy colours, namely browns and greens. Not only do these colours emphasize a connection with the natural world, but they are also less likely to stain.

Many other Pagan groups prefer ritual clothing modelled on pre-modern styles and decorated with traditional folk patterns, thus evoking both the pre-Christian past and a sense of ethnic or cultural identity. Consequently, the ceremonies of some more geographically focused Pagan groups, such as followers of Heathenry, Rodnovery or Romuva – movements

**PROFILE**
TOTEM
POLES

The traditional arts of the Pacific Northwest have long placed emphasis on wood carving, most recognizably in the form of totem poles, like those seen here in a Kwakiutl community in *c.* 1914. Probably emerging amid growing trade links with Europeans in the late 18th or early 19th century, they typically depict animals representing clan identities or scenes from myth and legend.

**BEAVER**
Beavers became a recurring clan emblem amid the establishment of the flourishing trade in beaver pelts during the first half of the 19th century. This beaver totem pole was photographed in Ketchikan, Alaska, USA.

**BEAR**
This is a Kwakiutl bear pole, carved by Henry Hunt in Victoria, Canada. Bear clans sometimes trace their ancestry to humans who mated with bears. In Pacific Northwest mythologies, bears often appear as humans.

**EAGLE**
Possessing many of the same traits as the mythological Thunderbird, the eagle is a noble bird, one who can both help and harm humans. This totem pole, carved by Beau Dick, is on Cormorant Island, Canada.

**RAVEN**
Raven can be both a hero and a trickster in the mythologies of the Pacific Northwest, having played a role in the creation of the world. This eagle detail features on a totem pole in Juneau, Alaska, USA.

**DZUNUKWA**
This example of a Dzunukwa totem pole is from Vancouver Island, Canada. Dzunukwas are considered to be dark-skinned female creatures with pursed lips that live in the woods and will sometimes steal children.

**SEA LION**
This front house post, used to support the main beam of a Haida home, depicts a sea lion, a species rarely used in totem pole designs. Some tribes of the Pacific Northwest consider the sea lion a source of hunting power.

*The tattooing practices
of several traditionally
non-Abrahamic societies,
such as the Māori (left) and
the Japanese (right), have
held particular fascination
for certain counter-cultural
groups in the West, including
modern Pagans.*

based on the pre-Christian traditions of Germanic, Slavic and Lithuanian peoples, respectively – often resemble meetings of historical re-enactors. By wearing such clothes, these practitioners hope to bring authenticity to their rituals and enhance a sense of continuity with their pre-Christian ancestors. Not all modern Pagans share this approach, though; many wear everyday contemporary clothing at their rituals.

* * *

Modern Pagans are a minority set apart from their Christian or non-religious neighbours. Consequently, many choose to wear something – usually a piece of jewelry, but sometimes clothing or a tattoo – through which they indicate their Pagan identity. Sometimes, this is worn to make a clear statement to everyone, proclaiming the wearer's religious affiliation publicly, but in other cases it is worn discreetly, communicating only to those who are themselves Pagans or are otherwise sympathetic.

The choice of symbol can indicate the specific Pagan religion of the wearer. The pentagram, or

**Wiccan Ritual**
*An American coven of Wiccans based in Hoopeston, Illinois, wear dark robes for their rituals.*

five-pointed star, is typically worn by Wiccans, both because of its associations with magical practice and its adoption as a common symbol of Wicca itself. Heathens will often wear modern versions of Thor's Mjölnir, while those inspired by ancient Egyptian religion will commonly bear an ankh, a symbol denoting life. Those wanting to convey their identity more surreptitiously may wear jewelry, clothing or tattoos featuring knotwork patterns inspired by the designs of early medieval northwest Europe. In rarer cases, symbols worn can indicate membership of a more specific group. Those initiated into Blue Star Wicca, for example, are often tattooed with a blue septagram, or seven-pointed star. Objects worn by modern Pagans can also be intended as amulets or talismans, sometimes dedicated to a particular purpose.

It is common to find certain aesthetic styles recurring within Pagan communities. Some Wiccans, for example, favour a 'witchy' aesthetic dominated by blacks and purples. A minority belong to the Goth subculture, which emerged out of Britain's post-punk milieu in the 1980s. Members identify themselves

## PROFILE
MODERN
PAGAN
SYMBOLS

Modern societies have become accustomed to the use of symbols to represent different religious identities, such as the Christian cross, the Jewish Star of David and the Muslim crescent moon and star. Contemporary Pagan religions have also adopted this practice, selecting symbols that bear specific connotations within particular belief systems. These symbols are typically drawn from the material culture of past societies, often borrowed from archaeological artefacts. A prominent example is Mjölnir, the hammer of the Norse god Thor, which was apparently worn as a pendant by his Scandinavian worshippers between the 9th and 11th centuries and that has been revived as the most prominent symbol of modern Heathenry. Many Heathens choose to wear this symbol on their body or otherwise display it on their property, thus reflecting how symbols can serve as an outward display of a person's religious identity.

*TRISKELE*
Based on patterns found carved into the rock at the Neolithic site of Newgrange in Ireland, the triskele is particularly popular among adherents of Celtic Reconstructionist Paganism.

*TRIQUETRA*
The three points of the triquetra have drawn the interest of Wiccans, thus inspiring the symbol's prominent use as a witches' emblem in American television show *Charmed*.

*VALKNUT*
Found on several early medieval artefacts from Northern Europe, the valknut has been embraced by Heathens, who often display it as a declaration of commitment to the god Odin.

*TRIPLE MOON*
Used largely by Wiccans, the Triple Moon symbol depicts the moon in its waxing, full and waning forms, thus symbolizing the Goddess as Maiden, Mother and Crone.

*AWEN*
Favoured by modern Druids, the awen symbol is often attributed to Iolo Morganwg, a Welsh antiquarian whose forged medieval documents have long influenced Druidry.

*SPIRAL GODDESS*
Influenced by prehistoric female figurines that have often been interpreted as depictions of a goddess, this figure is especially popular within the Goddess movement.

*PENTAGRAM*
The five-pointed pentagram has had many meanings in history, but for Wiccans it often represents unity of the five symbolic elements: earth, air, fire, water and spirit.

*SERPENT FLAG*
This serpentine flag is a symbol of Romuva, the religion inspired by the pre-Christian religion of the Lithuanians. It draws on ophidian imagery found in the country's folk art.

*ANKH*
The ankh is an ancient Egyptian symbol, utilized to symbolize life. Various modern Pagans now use it, especially followers of Kemetism, which venerates ancient Egyptian deities.

by wearing predominantly dark colours, and in a few cases openly describe their tradition as 'Goth Wicca'. Beards are common among Heathen men and convey an image of masculine ruggedness. Followers of these styles are drawing on long-standing visual portrayals that are deep-rooted in European culture, such as the bearded Viking warrior or the dark-clad witch. Not all practitioners of these traditions dress in this fashion, though, and some of those who do not are critical of what they regard as the clichéd clothing choices of their fellow Pagans.

Various social events provide opportunities to wear these styles. These include pub 'moots' or meet-ups, lectures in esoteric shops and – on a larger scale – Pagan festivals. Such occasions, bringing together tens if not hundreds of people, emerged in the USA during the 1970s. Although originally held in hotels, these festivals were, by the 1980s, increasingly taking place outdoors, often in rural areas – a set-up influenced by the ethos of rock festivals. For North American Pagans, these festivals became places where attendees could reject the norms of the outside world, often manifested by their choice of bodily adornment.

A medievalist aesthetic became common in festival spaces, with many individuals wearing flowing gowns and robes that would not look out of place at a Renaissance fair. Another aesthetic that influenced the Pagan festival scene was that of the Modern Primitive movement. Arising during the late 1980s and 1990s, the Modern Primitives drew upon body modification styles from so-called 'primitive' societies in constructing their own counter-cultural image. The Modern Primitive aesthetic placed great emphasis on tattooing and piercing, both of which became common adornments among North American Pagans. Although many Pagans enjoyed this style, concerns were raised that Modern Primitivism engages in cultural misappropriation – an issue that modern Pagans have had to navigate repeatedly when drawing inspiration from other non-Abrahamic religious traditions.

**Wiccan Ritual in England**
*The use of ritual nudity, robes, fire and the five-pointed pentagram features regularly in the ceremonies of Wiccan covens. This outdoor ceremony in England's Epping Forest, Essex, was photographed in 1994. Epping Forest has been a popular site among Pagan worshippers since Neolithic times.*

# JOURNEYING

THEY CAME TO A LAND
OF JOY, THE PLEASANT
LAWNS AND HAPPY SEATS
OF THE BLISSFUL GROVES.
HERE AN AMPLER ETHER
CLOTHES THE MEADS WITH
ROSEATE LIGHT, AND THEY
KNOW THEIR OWN SUN,
AND STARS OF THEIR OWN.

VIRGIL, AENEID, BOOK 6

TRANS. HENRY RUSHTON FAIRCLOUGH

Many societies have understood the realm of humanity as being just one among many, located alongside the realms of the gods and goddesses and of the ancestral dead. The boundaries between humanity's world and these others are not always impermeable. Many communities have believed that interaction between the realms is possible, either through contact between the living and the dead or through visionary journeys undertaken by ritual specialists.

**N**on-Abrahamic worldviews typically populate the cosmos with a plethora of different entities, each with their own powers, temperaments and experiences. Often, these 'other-than-human persons' are thought to reside in separate worlds parallel to that of humanity, creating a complex multilayered universe. Many societies have thought it possible to travel between these different realms, although the manner in which these journeys take place varies. In some tales, brave warriors travel between different realms as part of their epic quests. Elsewhere, certain ritual specialists are deemed capable of journeying between the worlds, at least in spirit form, to gain hidden knowledge from those that dwell there.

Nine worlds are found in Old Norse cosmology, situated around a cosmic ash tree, Yggdrasil. The roots of this tree covered not only the realm of humanity but also that of the *jötnar*, creatures who often fought the gods, and Hel, one of the realms of the dead. Journeying up and down the tree was a squirrel, Ratatoskr, who passed on messages between an eagle perched in its branches and a dragon, Níðhöggr, who chewed at its roots. Among the other Norse realms are Ásgarðr and Vanaheimr, homes to the two races of deities, and Álfheimr, the world of the elves.

Nine worlds also feature in the traditional beliefs of the Chukchi of Northeast Asia, although these realms are believed to be stacked, one above the other. A simpler notion of a three-tiered cosmos is found among the traditional beliefs of the Mapuche people of Chile and Argentina. For the Mapuche, the world of humanity, *mapu*, sits below the pure sky realm of *wenu mapu*, where both the gods and the spirits of the ancestors live. Below is the polluted underworld of *munche mapu*, home of the harmful *wekufe* spirits. The Mapuche believe that their ritual specialists, the *machi*, can travel between different realms while in a trance state. While doing so, the *machi* often clamber up a sturdy timber pole onto which notches have been carved. This pole is called the *rewe* and it is thought to be inhabited by a spirit from whom the *machi* receive their powers.

< *page 226*
Pierre Amédée Marcel-Béronneau, *Orpheus in Hades*, 1897
*In ancient Greek legend, the musician Orpheus descended into the underworld realm of Hades to rescue his wife, Eurydice.*

Arnold Böcklin, *Island of the Dead*, 1880–83

In these two versions of the same scene, Swiss painter Böcklin depicts the Island of the Dead, perhaps inspired by Classical pre-Christian accounts of the afterlife. The original work was commissioned by the artist's patron Marie Berna in memory of her late husband. The draped coffin and shrouded figure in the boat were added at her request.

# DECODING
YGGDRASIL

According to medieval Icelandic texts, the pre-Christian Norse perceived the cosmos as a tree called Yggdrasil, depicted below in Finnur Magnússon's 19th-century illustration. Yggdrasil is an ash tree that remains evergreen, and its name means 'Yggr's horse'. 'Yggr' is one of the names of the god Odin; the 'horse' is a possible reference to the gallows on which Odin hung, as told in one of the important myths about him.

## VEÐRFÖLNIR

Veðrfölnir is a hawk
who sits between the
eyes of the eagle atop
Yggdrasil. Little is
known of this creature,
who may represent
the eagle's wisdom.

1.

## EAGLE

An eagle, unnamed
in surviving sources,
perches in the tree's
branches. The eagle
argues with Níðhöggr,
the dragon who sits
far beneath him.

2.

## DÁINN, DVALINN, DUNEYRR AND DURAÞRÓR

Four stags graze on the
branches of Yggdrasil.
The names of two
of them, Dáinn and
Dvalinn, also appear as
dwarf names in Norse
mythology.

3.

## RATATOSKR

The squirrel Ratatoskr
runs up and down the ash
tree, delivering messages
between the eagle at the
top and Níðhöggr at the
bottom, sowing discord
between them.

4.

## NÍÐHÖGGR

A dragon of death,
Níðhöggr, lives beneath
the roots of Yggdrasil,
chewing on them.
Surviving sources
recount that he will
survive Ragnarök.

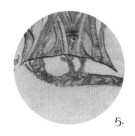

5.

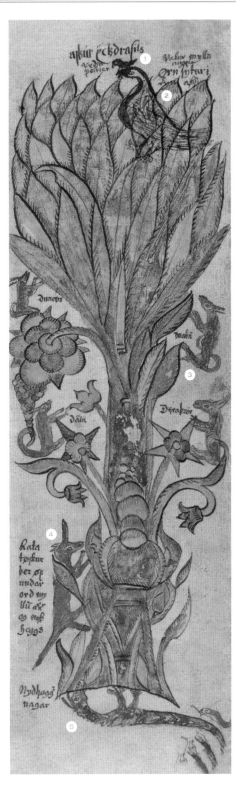

**Stone Age Rock Art from Tanzania**

*Prehistoric rock art can be difficult to interpret accurately. In the early 20th century it was common for European scholars to assume that such paintings and carvings (the latter called petroglyphs) were created to compel prey animals to appear before the community's hunters. Later scholarship has offered alternative explanations,*

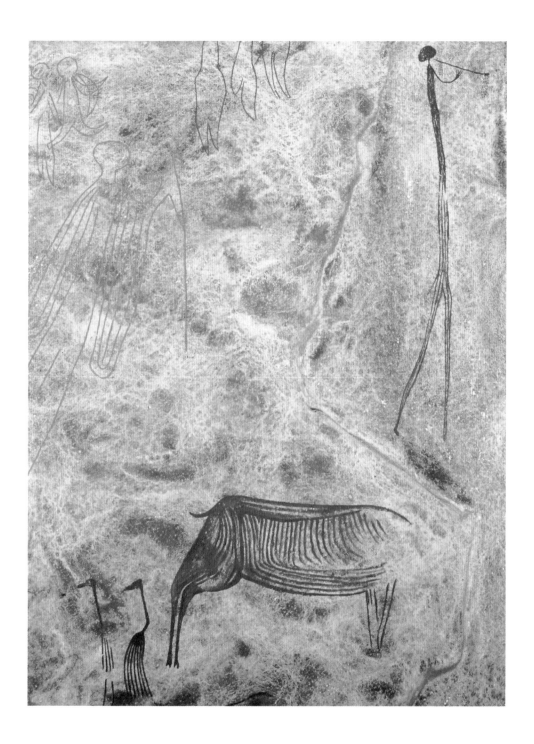

*often informed by ethnographic research. Some archaeologists have suggested that these artworks from Tanzania, for example, are the product of ritual dances designed to induce trance states. The dominant circular motif is interpreted as representing a visual hallucination known as a phosphene. It is surrounded by depictions of dancers.*

Similar rituals in which people believed that they travelled in spirit form through multiple realms were found among various traditional societies of North Asia. An ethnographic account of an Evenk ritualist collected in 1931, for example, recounts how his spirit journey relied on an animal double. These entities were commonly found among Evenk and Enet communities and usually took the form of a reindeer or boar. As part of a ritual to determine why his patient was sick, the Evenk ritualist drummed and sang invocatory songs calling on the spirits. The ritualist then described how he could see his animal double travelling to other realms, encountering both an ancestral spirit and the supreme deity, before eventually discovering the cause of his patient's ailment. Elsewhere in North Asia, these visionary journeys might serve purposes other than healing. Among the Nanai people, for example, the *kasanti* ritualists were tasked with escorting the souls of the deceased to the lands of the dead.

Visionary experiences have also been commonplace among the ritual specialists of Amazonia, where they are often facilitated through consuming *ayahuasca*, a psychoactive brew comprising various indigenous plants. While there is much variation in their practices, these specialists often journey into the rainforest to consume *ayahuasca*, experiencing visions in which they meet with the spirits of different plant species.

**Yup'ik Ritual Material**
*The mask (left) and dance object (right) are from the Yup'ik people of Alaska, c. 1900. The symbolism of these works reflects the importance of the hunt to traditional Yup'ik subsistence.*

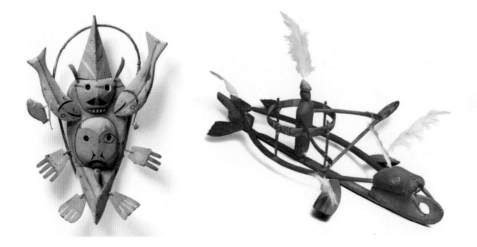

These spirits educate them about the healing values
of their plants and also teach them ritual songs,
typically called *icaros*. Since the 1990s, international
interest in this process has fuelled a growing tourist
industry, with Westerners travelling to Amazonia
to experience the *ayahuasca* ceremony and also
introducing the psychoactive substance to their
own nations.

Certain speakers of the Tungusic languages of
North Asia referred to some of their ritual specialists
as *shamans*, a term increasingly adopted by European
languages after being introduced to them from the late
17th century onward. The term 'shamanism' has since
been applied widely, not only to North Asian societies
but also to communities across the world. In turn, it
has been given various, often conflicting, meanings.
Sometimes the word has been used to characterize
those who journey into another spiritual realm to
achieve a particular task, but elsewhere it has been
employed more broadly to describe anyone contacting
spirits while in an altered state of consciousness, such

**Altai Ritual Specialist**   *Taken by the ethnographer V. V. Sapozhnikov during his expeditions to Russia's Altai Mountains in the 1890s, this photograph depicts a ritual specialist from an Altai community. Dressed in a special outfit, the ritualist beats a drum during their performance; among Altaian peoples, the idea of the drum as a steed in visionary journeys was widespread.*

as the *mudang* ritualists of Korea. Like 'paganism' itself, 'shamanism' is a problematic word.

By the latter half of the 20th century, ethnographic accounts of ritual specialists undergoing visionary journeys in areas such as North Asia and Amazonia were inspiring Westerners to attempt similar practices. The result was Neo-Shamanism or Western Shamanism, a new religious milieu associated especially with American anthropologist and author Michael Harner (1929–2018). Neo-Shamans typically use chanting and music, particularly the beat of the drum, to enter trance states, often for the purposes of personal development and healing. Neo-Shamanism heavily overlaps modern Paganism, with many practitioners combining their visionary journeys with new religions focused on the deities of Europe's pre-Christian traditions. Modern Heathens have, for example, drawn on medieval accounts of *seiðr* to construct new ritual systems strongly influenced by Neo-Shamanism. Modern Heathen *seiðr* workers often use chanting and drumming to cultivate an altered state of consciousness in which they visualize themselves journeying to Norse mythological realms, such as Hel. It is in these realms that they seek wisdom and advice from gods, goddesses and other supernatural entities such as elves.

\* \* \*

One of the realms that has preoccupied people around the world is the afterlife. Many different visions of this have been set forth, often impacting how communities dispose of their dead. The considerable effort that ancient Egyptians made in burying many of their deceased, especially their kings, has meant that more is known about attitudes to death in ancient Egyptian society than about many other facets of their religion. While perceptions of the afterlife undoubtedly varied over the course of ancient Egyptian history, a common belief was that the deceased would be judged on how they had acted during life. As portrayed on papyrus illustrations – for example in the *Book of the Dead*, which came into use during the 2nd millennium BC – this judgment was overseen by the god Osiris. The

## PROFILE
MUSICAL
INSTRUMENTS

Whether it involves singing, clapping or the playing of instruments, music is a regular feature of religious ceremonies. Sometimes, music can be used to praise divinities or to invoke their presence at a ceremony. It can also help to induce altered states of consciousness in either a ritual specialist or the congregation. This is why instruments can be found in places of worship such as the Japanese *jinja*, seen here in a lacquer painting titled *Drum for Gagaku Dance* (1882).

*SAAMI DRUM*
Among the Saami of Northern Europe, drums decorated with symbolic images were key ritual tools of specialists called *noaidi*. Many were destroyed during Christianization efforts, but this 17th-century example survives.

*DIDGERIDOO*
Found among various Aboriginal groups in northern parts of Australia, the didgeridoo is used to accompany a range of different rituals, including ceremonial dances.

*HAIDA RATTLE*
Among the Haida and other Pacific Northwest peoples, the rattle carved with a spirit's face is often used in ceremonial dances. This 19th-century example potentially depicts a grinning bear spirit.

*TAAL*
These handheld cymbals have many uses in Indian music. In Hindu contexts, they are widely used during devotional songs intended to praise particular deities such as Krishna.

*VODOU ASSON*
Usually made from a calabash gourd, as in this example that also features beads and snake vertebrae, the *asson* is a rattle used in Haitian Vodou to call *lwa* spirits to attend ceremonies.

*BATÁ*
The *batá* is a style of drum with West African origins. In the Cuban religion of Santería, it is used in ceremonies designed to facilitate the possession of a dancer by an *orisha*.

**Egyptian Afterlife**
*A deceased person faces judgment in this scene from the* Book of the Dead, *preserved on an ancient Egyptian papyrus dating from the 19th dynasty.*

heart of the deceased was weighed against the white feather of Ma'at. If the heart and feather weighed the same, the dead person was ruled to have lived a good life and was allowed to enter a paradisal afterlife, the Field of Reeds. If the heart was heavier than the feather, it revealed that the person had led an unvirtuous life. Their heart would be devoured by a fearsome creature with a crocodile's head, thus obliterating their soul forever.

An insight into the nature of the afterlife as understood by the ancient Greeks can be found in the *Odyssey*, in which the hero Odysseus travels to the entrance of the underworld to speak with the dead seer Tiresias. There, he encounters other spirits of the deceased, who recall many of the sights in the underworld, including the punishment of figures who have displeased the gods. Tityos, for example, has two vultures pecking at his liver, while Tantalus is plagued with continual hunger and thirst, unable to reach the food and water placed before him. In the *Aeneid*, an epic poem written by Roman author Virgil (70–19 BC) in the 1st century BC, Aeneas, the Trojan protagonist, also explores the underworld. Accompanied by an oracle of Apollo, the Sibyl, Aeneas enters the underworld by passing over the River Acheron and then sedating the three-headed guard dog Cerberus. Once in the afterlife, Aeneas observes its division into two very different parts: a place of torment for those who had lived badly by offending the gods or disrespecting their family, and the estate of the blessed, an idyllic realm lit by

Adolf Hirémy-Hirschl,
*Souls on the Banks of
the Acheron*, 1898
*This Symbolist painting depicts
the ancient Greek god Hermes
in his role as psychopomp,
guiding the dead to the afterlife.*

sun and starshine, where the virtuous dead enjoy dancing and games serenaded by the bard Orpheus.

The continuing relationship between the living and the dead has been a central concern for some communities. The ongoing presence of the ancestors among the living is a recurring idea among Polynesian peoples, as can be seen through the *wharenui* buildings that represent a material manifestation of the ancestors for traditional Māori people. Other societies have specific objects that symbolize the ancestral presence. The Ibo of West Africa traditionally embody their ancestors in timber posts that are brought inside the house and given libations of food and wine. Also representing the Ibo ancestors is the *ofo*, a stick that the head of the family wields as a symbol of their authority. In some cases, the ancestors may be thought to visit the living on a more sporadic basis. The Mapuche, for example, believe that ancestors will return to haunt those who have failed to properly acknowledge them. This is not done out of malice, but rather to remind the living of their obligations.

Some societies have not presumed that the afterlife is a permanent abode, instead believing that each soul

**1.**

**2.**

**3.**

**4.**

## DECODING
## AENEAS IN THE
## UNDERWORLD

In the 1st century BC, the Roman writer
Virgil created his epic poem the *Aeneid*.
Its protagonist, the Trojan Aeneas,
travelled to the underworld to find his
deceased father. Carrying the golden
bough and accompanied by an oracle
of Apollo, the Cumaean Sibyl, he passed
through a cave in the Euboean Rock
and travelled over the River Acheron
into Tartarus, there witnessing the
torture of miscreants. The scene
later inspired this artistic depiction
from Flemish artist Jan Brueghel the
Younger, titled *Aeneas and the Sibyl
in the Underworld* (1630s).

1. The entrance through the Euboean Rock
2. River Acheron
3. The Sibyl
4. Aeneas
5. The Golden Bough
6. The wicked being punished in Tartarus
7. Mutilated bodies of the dead

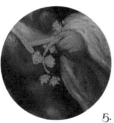

5.

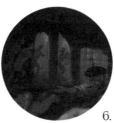

6.

7.

**Yama**

*Yama, the lord of death in various Hindu and Buddhist mythologies, holds the wheel of life, depicting the various realms into which people can be reborn.*

exists in a cycle of reincarnation. Greco-Roman writers such as Julius Caesar and Diodorus Siculus (*c.* 90–*c.* 20 BC) claimed that such a belief was held by the druids, ritual specialists active in parts of Iron Age Western Europe. The accuracy of these claims is uncertain, and if Iron Age European communities did believe in reincarnation, it is unclear if they thought it was governed by any moral force and whether a human soul would always be reborn in a human body. Today, belief in reincarnation is widespread in South and East Asian religions, such as Hinduism, where souls are thought to proceed in an ongoing cycle of reincarnation that encompasses many living species. The status of a soul's rebirth is impacted by their actions in the preceding life. For Hindus, reincarnation is not necessarily eternal, but can be escaped through spiritual release, or *moksha*. Belief in reincarnation has spread rapidly in Western countries over the past century, even being adopted by some Christians.

There are many ways of dealing with the dead. Common approaches include cremation and inhumation, but in other contexts bodies have

**Crow Burial Platform**

*This burial platform, photographed in c. 1908, carries a deceased member of the Crow community of the North American Plains.*

been deliberately left for animals to devour or have been de-fleshed and then placed in a special location. Some societies have even kept their dead within the domestic area. Although few retain their pre-Christian religion, many Torajan people of Sulawesi, Indonesia, for example, still continue the traditional practice of keeping the desiccated bodies of their relatives in their homes. Other communities have seen death as a source of impurity and have tried to distance themselves from it. The ancient Romans forbade the burial or burning of the dead inside the city walls. Today, an attempt to distance the living from the dead can still be seen among the Navajo and in Japanese Shinto, where people exposed to corpses must often undergo purification rituals.

In a few cases, the way in which a body is dealt with strongly implies the notion of a journey to the afterlife. This is very evident in ancient Egyptian burial practices, where great care was taken in mummifying the deceased and placing grave goods with them, something traditionally interpreted as material

## PROFILE
AFTERLIFE
WORLDS

Many societies conceive of an afterlife, the nature of which is impacted by how a person lives their life and how they die. Various myths recount the journey to the afterlife. Old Norse myth, for example, discusses valkyries taking those slain in battle to Valhalla, a subject re-imagined in Edward Robert Hughes' *Dream Idyll (A Valkyrie)* from 1902. The afterlife is not always wholly separate from our world, and many communities pursue ongoing interaction with its denizens.

**DIYU**

In traditional Chinese mythology, *Diyu* is a realm where spirits of the deceased may go and face punishment for misdemeanours perpetrated in life, prior to them being reborn in a new body.

**MESOPOTAMIAN UNDERWORLD**

This seal (2600–2300 BC) may depict the Mesopotamian myth of how the god Demuzid was forced into the dark underworld and tortured there for half a year.

**TERRACOTTA ARMY**

In *c.* 209–10 BC, Chinese Emperor Shi Huangdi was buried with thousands of terracotta warrior figures, which were perhaps intended to serve him in the afterlife.

**HADES**

Commonly called Hades after the god who oversaw it, pictured here with his wife Persephone, the ancient Greek afterlife is an underworld. Only a few heroes were able to visit this realm and then return to the living world.

**BURIAL MOUND**

In medieval Scandinavian folklore, the *draugr* is a spirit who dwelt within the burial mound. This suggests that not all those who die pass on into an afterlife realm, instead remaining to haunt our world.

**FIELD OF REEDS**

The Field of Reeds, or A'aru, pictured here in a facsimile of a 13th-century tomb painting, is an ancient Egyptian afterlife. It was only for those who had been judged worthy during the 'weighing of the heart' ceremony.

required for the next world. Paintings and texts on the walls of the tomb helped guide the deceased on their journey. Another clear example of this is seen among the linguistically Germanic societies of early medieval Europe, where members of the elite were sometimes given lavish burials inside ships. Among the best-known examples are the 7th-century burial at Sutton Hoo, England and the probably 9th-century burial at Oseberg, Norway. The Old English poem *Beowulf* recounts one deceased leader being set out to sea aboard a boat, while the Arab traveller Ibn' Fadlan (*c.* 879– *c.* 960) described a burial inside a ship that was then set ablaze.

Modern Pagan funerals typically operate within the legal restrictions of Western countries and thus bear similarities with mainstream Western funeral practices, albeit with the choice of readings, prayers and sermons reflecting modern Pagan beliefs. Some practitioners favour a so-called 'natural burial', in which the body is not embalmed but placed within a biodegradable coffin, thus minimizing its harmful environmental impact. A few specialist Pagan burial areas have been established. Part of the Gufunes Cemetery near Reykjavik, Iceland, is set aside for Heathen burials. Sometimes, a grave might reflect the deceased's Pagan identity. In the USA, military headstones can now feature symbols, including a pentagram for Wiccans, Thor's hammer for Heathens and an Awen symbol for Druids.

Beliefs about life after death vary among modern Pagans. Many believe in reincarnation; others in an afterlife realm such as Valhalla or the Summerland. Some reject the idea of an incorporeal soul altogether. Various groups place emphasis on honouring their ancestors, while spirit mediumship – often influenced by Spiritualism – is also embraced by some Pagans. Typically, however, the afterlife is a topic of far less interest to modern Pagans than it is to practitioners of Abrahamic religions. In general, modern Pagan religions are world-affirming, placing their emphasis on celebrating life, building good relationships and making the most of the here and now.

**Hermann Hendrich,**
***Wotan Waits in Valhalla***
***for the End with His***
***Broken Spear,*** 1906

*German painter Hendrich's early 20th-century interpretation of the Germanic god*
*Wotan (known in Old Norse as Odin) shows him sitting in his afterlife realm, Valhalla.*
*There, he waits for the end of the world - Ragnarök. Ragnarök involves the death of*
*a number of important gods, not only Odin but also Thor, Freyr and Loki, for example.*

# FURTHER READING

## CONCEPTUAL HISTORY OF PAGANISM

Bull, Malcolm, *The Mirror of the Gods: How Renaissance Artists Rediscovered the Pagan Gods* (Oxford: Oxford University Press, 2005).

Chuvin, Pierre, *A Chronicle of the Last Pagans* (Cambridge, MA: Harvard University Press, 1990).

Davies, Owen, *Paganism: A Very Short Introduction* (Oxford: Oxford University Press, 2011).

Fletcher, Richard, *The Conversion of Europe: From Paganism to Christianity, 371–1386 AD* (London: HarperCollins, 1997).

Godwin, Joscelyn, *The Pagan Dream of the Renaissance* (Grand Rapids, MI: Phanes Press, 2002).

Lane Fox, Robin, *Pagans and Christians: In the Mediterranean World from the Second Century AD to the Conversion of Constantine* (London: Viking, 1986).

O'Donnell, James J., 'Paganus', *Classical Folia,* 31 (1977), 163–169.
*Pagans: The End of Traditional Religion and the Rise of Christianity* (New York: HarperCollins, 2015).

Seznec, Jean, *The Survival of the Pagan Gods: The Mythological Tradition and its Place in Renaissance Humanism and Art* (Princeton, NJ: Princeton University Press, 1953).

York, Michael, *Pagan Theology: Paganism as a World Religion* (New York: New York University Press, 2003).

## THE ANCIENT WORLD

Bottéro, Jean, *Religion in Ancient Mesopotamia* (Chicago, IL: University of Chicago Press, 2001).

Burkert, Walter, *Greek Religion* (Malden, MA: Blackwell, 1985).

Dowden, Ken, *European Paganism: The Realities of Cult from Antiquity to the Middle Ages* (London: Routledge, 2000).

DuBois, Thomas A., *Nordic Religions in the Viking Age* (Philadelphia: University of Pennsylvania Press, 1999).

Ellis Davidson, H. E., *Gods and Myths of Northern Europe* (London: Penguin, 1964).

Kalik, Judith and Alexander Uchitel, *Slavic Gods and Heroes* (London: Routledge, 2019).

Quirke, Stephen, *Exploring Religion in Ancient Egypt* (Chichester: Wiley Blackwell, 2015).

Rives, James B., *Religion in the Roman Empire* (Malden, MA: Blackwell, 2007).

Warrior, Valerie M., *Roman Religion* (Cambridge: Cambridge University Press, 2006).

Williams, Mark, *Ireland's Immortals: A History of the Gods of Irish Myth* (Princeton: Princeton University Press, 2016).

## AFRICAN AND AFRICAN DIASPORIC RELIGION

Bascom, William, *Ifa Divination: Communication between Gods and Men in West Africa* (Bloomington, IN: Indiana University Press, 1969).

Brown, Karen McCarthy, *Mama Lola: A Vodou Priestess in Brooklyn*, revised edition (Berkeley, CA: University of California Press, 2001).

Clark, Mary Ann, *Santería: Correcting the Myths and Uncovering the Realities of a Growing Religion* (Westport, CT: Praeger, 2007).

Evans-Pritchard, E. E., *Nuer Religion* (Oxford: Clarendon Press, 1956).

Johnson, Paul Christopher, *Secrets, Gossip, and Gods: The Transformation of Brazilian Candomblé* (Oxford: Oxford University Press, 2002).

Mair, Lucy, *Witchcraft* (London: Weidenfeld and Nicolson, 1969).

Mbiti, John S., *Introduction to African Religion*, second edition (Nairobi: East African Educational Publishers, 1992).

Middleton, John, *Lugbara Religion: Ritual and Authority among an East African People* (London: Oxford University Press, 1960).

Parrinder, Geoffrey, *West African Religion*, revised edition (London: Epworth Press, 1961).

Peek, Philip M. (ed.), *African Divination Systems: Ways of Knowing* (Bloomington, IN: Indiana University Press, 1991).

## ASIAN RELIGIONS

Baldick, Julian, *Animal and Shaman: Ancient Religions of Central Asia* (London: I.B. Tauris, 2000).

Cali, Joseph and John Dougill, *Shinto Shrines: A Guide to the Sacred Sites of Japan's Ancient Religion* (Honolulu, HI: University of Hawai'i Press, 2013).

Eck, Diana L., *Darśan: Seeing the Divine Image in India*, third edition (New York: Columbia University Press, 1998).

Flood, Gavin, *An Introduction to Hinduism* (Cambridge: Cambridge University Press, 1996).

Fowler, Jeaneane and Merv Fowler, *Chinese Religions: Beliefs and Practices* (Brighton: Sussex Academic Press, 2008).

Haberman, David L., *People Trees: Worship of Trees in Northern India* (Oxford: Oxford University Press, 2013).

Hutton, Ronald, *Shamans: Siberian Spirituality and the Western Imagination* (London: Hambledon and London, 2001).

Kim, Chongho, *Korean Shamanism: The Cultural Paradox* (Aldershot: Ashgate, 2003).

Michell, George, *The Hindu Temple: An Introduction to its Meanings and Forms* (London: Paul Elek, 1977).

Nelson, John K., *A Year in the Life of a Shinto Shrine* (Seattle, WA: University of Washington Press, 1996).

## NATIVE AMERICAN RELIGIONS

Amoss, Pamela, *Coast Salish Spirit Dancing: The Survival of an Ancestral Religion* (Seattle, WA: University of Washington Press, 1978).

Bacigalupo, Ana Mariella, *Shamans of the Foye Tree: Gender, Power, and Healing among Chilean Mapuche* (Austin, TX: University of Texas Press, 2007).

Beyer, Stephan V., *Singing to the Plants: A Guide to Mestizo Shamanism in the Upper Amazon* (Albuquerque, NM: University of New Mexico Press, 2009).

Brundage, Burr Cartwright, *The Fifth Sun: Aztec Gods, Aztec World* (Austin, TX: University of Texas Press, 1979).

Carrasco, David, *Religions of Mesoamerica*, second edition (Long Grove, IL: Waveland Press, 2014).

Crawford, Suzanne J., *Native American Religious Traditions* (Upper Saddle River, NJ: Prentice Hall, 2007).

Feraca, Stephen E., *Wakinyan: Lakota Religion in the Twentieth Century* (Lincoln, NE: University of Nebraska Press, 1998).

Hart, Thomas, *The Ancient Spirituality of the Modern Maya* (Albuquerque, NM: University of New Mexico Press, 2008).

Hultkrantz, Åke, *The Religions of the American Indians* (Berkeley, CA: University of California Press, 1979).

Loftin, John D., *Religion and Hopi Life*, second edition (Bloomington, IN: Indiana University Press, 2003).

## OCEANIC RELIGIONS

Aerts, Theo, *Traditional Religion in Melanesia* (Port Moresby: University of Papua New Guinea Press, 2012).

Charlesworth, Max, Françoise Dussart, and Howard Morphy (eds), *Aboriginal Religions in Australia: An Anthology of Recent Writings* (Aldershot: Ashgate, 2005).

Firth, Raymond, *Tikopia Ritual and Belief* (London: George Allen and Unwin, 1967).

Mead, Sidney Moko, *Landmarks, Bridges and Visions: Aspects of Maori Culture* (Wellington: Victoria University Press, 1997).

Rose, Deborah, *Dingo Makes Us Human: Life and Land in an Australian Aboriginal Culture* (Cambridge: Cambridge University Press, 2000).

Shortland, Edward, *Maori Religion and Mythology* (London: Longmans, Green and Company, 1882).

Stanner, W. E. H., *On Aboriginal Religion* (Sydney: Sydney University Press, 2014).

Trompf, G. W., *Melanesian Religion* (Cambridge: Cambridge University Press, 1994).

Valeri, Valerio, *Kingship and Sacrifice: Ritual and Society in Ancient Hawaii* (Chicago: Chicago University Press, 1985).

Williamson, Robert Wood, *Religion and Social Organization in Central Polynesia* (Cambridge: Cambridge University Press, 1937).

## MODERN PAGANISM

Aitamurto, Kaarina, *Paganism, Traditionalism, Nationalism: Narratives of Russian Rodnoverie* (London: Routledge, 2016).

Blain, Jenny, *Nine Worlds of Seid-Magic: Ecstasy and Neo-Shamanism in North European Paganism* (London: Routledge, 2002).

Calico, Jefferson F., *Being Viking: Heathenism in Contemporary America* (Sheffield: Equinox, 2018).

Clifton, Chas S., *Her Hidden Children: The Rise of Wicca and Paganism in America* (Lanham, MD: AltaMira Press, 2006).

Doyle White, Ethan, *Wicca: History, Belief, and Community in Modern Pagan Witchcraft* (Brighton: Sussex Academic Press, 2016).

Eller, Cynthia, *The Myth of Matriarchal Prehistory: Why an Invented Past Won't Give Women a Future* (Boston: Beacon Press, 2000).

Harvey, Graham, *Listening People, Speaking Earth: Contemporary Paganism*, second edition (London: Hurst and Company, 2007).

Hutton, Ronald, *The Triumph of the Moon: A History of Modern Pagan Witchcraft* (Oxford: Oxford University Press, 1999).

Lesiv, Mariya, *The Return of Ancestral Gods: Modern Ukrainian Paganism as an Alternative Vision for a Nation* (Montreal: McGill-Queen's University Press, 2013).

Magliocco, Sabina, *Neo-Pagan Sacred Art and Altars: Making Things Whole* (Jackson, MI: University Press of Mississippi, 2001).

# SOURCES OF
# ILLUSTRATIONS

**a** = above, **b** = below, **c** = centre, **l** = left, **r** = right

**Front cover** © Art Gallery of South Australia, Adelaide /Gift of the Right Honourable, the Earl of Kintore 1893/ Bridgeman Images
**Back cover and spine** © Swedish National Art Museum/ Bridgeman Images

**1** Karen Fuller/Alamy Stock Photo; **2** © Museo Lázaro Galdiano, Madrid; **4** US National Archives and Records Administration; **6–7** © Swedish National Art Museum/Bridgeman Images; **8–9** Chris Moorhouse/Evening Standard/Hulton Archive/ Getty Images; **10** Werner Forman/Universal Images Group/ Getty Images; **13** Virginia Lupu; **14l** The J. Paul Getty Museum, Los Angeles; **14c** The J. Paul Getty Museum, Los Angeles, gift of Barbara and Lawrence Fleischman; **14r** The J. Paul Getty Museum, Los Angeles; **15** Mike Davis; **16** Heritage Image Partnership Ltd/Alamy Stock Photo; **17l** akg-images; **17r** North Wind Picture Archives/Alamy Stock Photo; **18, 19** Fine Art Images/Heritage Images/Getty Images; **20** Heritage Image Partnership Ltd/Alamy Stock Photo; **21l** © The Trustees of the British Museum; **21r** Heritage Art/Heritage Images via Getty Images; **23** Peter Eastland/Alamy Stock Photo; **24** Konstantin Zavrazhin/Getty Images; **27** GL Archive/Alamy Stock Photo; **28** Heritage Image Partnership Ltd/Alamy Stock Photo; **31al** The Metropolitan Museum of Art, New York, Rogers Fund, 1948; **31ar** The Metropolitan Museum of Art, New York, purchase, Joseph Pulitzer bequest fund, 1955; **31bl** The Metropolitan Museum of Art, New York, purchase, Lila Acheson Wallace gift, 1991; **31br** The Metropolitan Museum of Art, New York, Rogers Fund, 1912; **32–33** David Silverman/ Getty Images; **34l** Pictures From History/Universal Images Group via Getty Images; **34c** Pictures From History/Bridgeman Images; **34r** The Picture Art Collection/Alamy Stock Photo; **35l** © The Trustees of the British Museum; **35r** nyaa_birdies_ perch; **36** The Metropolitan Museum of Art, New York, purchase, anonymous gift, 2013; **37l, 37c** The Metropolitan Museum of Art, New York, The Crosby Brown Collection of Musical Instruments, 1889; **37r** The Metropolitan Museum of Art, New York, The Charles and Valerie Diker Collection of Native American Art, gift of Charles and Valerie Diker, 2019; **38, 39al** The Metropolitan Museum of Art, New York, gift of James Douglas, 1890; **39ac** The Metropolitan Museum of Art, New York, Theodore M. Davis Collection, bequest of Theodore M. Davis, 1915; **39ar** The Metropolitan Museum of Art, New York, purchase, Edward S. Harkness gift, 1926; **39bl** Rama; **39bc, 39br** The Metropolitan Museum of Art, New York, gift of Darius Ogden Mills, 1904; **40l** The Metropolitan Museum of Art, New York, purchase, Joseph Pulitzer bequest, 1952; **40r** The Metropolitan Museum of Art, New York, purchase, Edward S. Harkness gift, 1926; **41l** Creative Touch Imaging Ltd/ NurPhoto via Getty Images; **41c** Godong/Universal Images Group via Getty Images; **41r** Creative Touch Imaging Ltd/ NurPhoto via Getty Images; **42l** The Metropolitan Museum of Art, New York, gift of Doris Wiener, in honour of Steven Kossak, 2000; **42c** The Metropolitan Museum of Art, New York, gift of Mark Baron and Elise Boisanté, 2012; **42r** Sepia Times/Universal Images Group via Getty Images; **43al** The Metropolitan Museum of Art, New York, purchase, gift of Mrs William J. Calhoun, by exchange, 2013; **43ac** The Metropolitan Museum of Art, New York, purchase, Robert and Bobbie Falk philanthropic fund gift, 2021; **43ar** The Metropolitan Museum of Art, New York, purchase, Friends of Asian Art gift, 2021; **43bl** Sepia Times/Universal Images Group via Getty Images; **43bc** The Metropolitan Museum of Art, New York, purchase, Rogers Fund, Evelyn Kranes Kossak gift and funds from various donors, 2000; **43br** Sepia Times/Universal Images Group via Getty Images; **44** DEA/G. Dagli Orti/DeAgostini via Getty Images; **45** PHAS/Universal Images Group via Getty Images; **46–47a** Fine Art Images/Heritage Images via Getty Images; **46bl, 46bc, 46br** Pictures From History/Universal Images Group via Getty Images; **47bl** AF Fotografie/Alamy Stock Photo; **47bc, 47br** Historica Graphica Collection/Heritage Images/Getty Images; **48** The Metropolitan Museum of Art, New York, Rogers Fund, 1916; **49** Mick Sharp/Alamy Stock Photo; **50** Werner Forman/Universal Images Group/Getty

Images; **51al, 51ac, 51ar, 51bl, 51bc** Orisha Statues (Obatala, Elegua, Oshun,Yemaya, Shango); **51br** Wellcome Collection, London; **52** © National Museums Liverpool/Bridgeman Images; **55** The Metropolitan Museum of Art, New York, bequest of William H. Herriman, 1920; **56–57** Fine Art Images/ Heritage Images/Getty Images; **58** © The Trustees of the British Museum; **59** Philadelphia Museum of Art, The George W. Elkins Collection, 1924; **60** The Metropolitan Museum of Art, New York, Fletcher Fund, 1956; **61al** Album/Alamy Stock Photo; **61ac** Fine Art Images/Heritage Images via Getty Images; **61ar** Auk Archive/Alamy Stock Photo; **61bl** incamerastock/ Alamy Stock Photo; **61bc** Heritage Image Partnership Ltd/ Alamy Stock Photo; **61br** Gavin Hamilton, *Achilles Lamenting the Death of Patroclus*, National Galleries of Scotland, purchased 1976; **62** Marc Pachow; **63** The Metropolitan Museum of Art, New York, Mary Griggs Burke Collection, gift of the Mary and Jackson Burke Foundation, 2015; **64al, 64ac, 64ar** The Metropolitan Museum of Art, New York, gift of Felix M. Warburg and his family, 1941; **64bl** Heritage Art/Heritage Images via Getty Images; **64bc** The Metropolitan Museum of Art, New York, gift of Felix M. Warburg and his family, 1941; **64br** ZU_09/ Getty Images; **65al** Heritage Art/Heritage Images via Getty Images; **65ac** The Metropolitan Museum of Art, New York, bequest of Phyllis Massar, 2011; **65ar** © The Trustees of the British Museum; **65bl** The Metropolitan Museum of Art, New York, gift of Felix M. Warburg and his family, 1941; **65bc** The Metropolitan Museum of Art, New York, bequest of Grace M. Pugh, 1985; **65br** The Metropolitan Museum of Art, New York, gift of Henry Walters, 1917; **66** Ivy Close Images/ Alamy Stock Photo; **67** Sepia Times/Universal Images Group via Getty Images; **68** Fine Art Images/Heritage Images/Getty Images; **69al** Ola Myrin, Statens historiska museum/SHM; **69ac** PHAS/Universal Images Group via Getty Images; **69ar** Ola Myrin, Statens historiska museum/SHM; **69bl** M Dixon/ Print Collector/Getty Images; **69bc** Gunnar Creutz; **69br** Scott Gunn; **70** The Metropolitan Museum of Art, New York, David Hunter McAlpin fund, 1952; **73** The Metropolitan Museum of Art, New York, gift of Norbert Schimmel Trust, 1989; **74** Gavin Hellier/Alamy Stock Photo; **77** The Metropolitan Museum of Art, New York; **78** Luigi Spina/Electa/Mondadori Portfolio; **79** The Art Institute of Chicago, Potter Palmer Collection; **80** Luisa Ricciarini/Bridgeman Images; **81al** H. V. Hess, *Engleder, Vaterländische Geschichtsbilder nach Orginalen in den königlichen Museen*, Munich: Piloty and Loehle, 1911; **81ac** ZU_09/Getty Images; **81ar** Wellcome Collection, London; **81bl** The Metropolitan Museum of Art, New York, gift of Mrs Carll Tucker, 1962; **81bc** Matthew W. Stirling, *Stone Monuments of Southern Mexico*, bulletin no. 138, Washington: Smithsonian Institution, Bureau of American Ethnology, 1943; **81br** Gainew Gallery/Alamy Stock Photo; **82** Heritage Arts/Heritage Images via Getty Images; **83** The New York Public Library; **84** The Metropolitan Museum of Art, New York, purchase, Fletcher Fund and Joseph E. Hotung and Michael and Danielle Rosenberg gifts, 1989; **85al** The Metropolitan Museum of Art, New York, Rogers Fund, 1914; **85ac** Sepia Times/Universal Images Group via Getty Images; **85ar** G. Nimatallah/ DeAgostini via Getty Images; **85bl** Thierry Perrin/HOA-QUI/ Gamma-Rapho via Getty Images; **85bc** Joppi/Alamy Stock Photo; **85br** snapshot-photography/T Seeliger/Shutterstock; **86l** Bibi Saint-Pol; **86r** Granger/Bridgeman Images; **87l** Diego Grandi/Alamy Stock Photo; **87r** Elena Chaykina/Alamy Stock Photo; **88–89a** Universal Images Group via Getty Images; **88bl, 88bc** Sepia Times/Universal Images Group via Getty Images; **88br** Leemage/Corbis via Getty Images; **89bl** Juliet Highet/ArkReligion.com/Alamy Stock Photo; **89bc** Robert Rosenblum/Alamy Stock Photo; **89br** Liam Bennett/Alamy Stock Photo; **90–91** Robert Nickelsberg/ Liaison; **92** Wellcome Collection, London; **94al** Florilegius/ Alamy Stock Photo; **94bl** Historic Images/Alamy Stock Photo; **94br** EvergreenPlanet/Shutterstock; **95al** Dorling Kindersley Ltd/Alamy Stock Photo; **95ar** plantgenera.org; **95cl** Lorenzo Rossi/Alamy Stock Photo; **95cr** Florilegius/Alamy Stock Photo; **95bl** Jiri Hera/Shutterstock; **95cr** Florilegius/Alamy Stock Photo; **96** Oberon Zell, www.TheMillennialGaia.com; **97** Heritage Image Partnership Ltd/Alamy Stock Photo; **98** Art Media/Print Collector/Getty Images; **99al** Fine Art Images/Heritage Images via Getty Images; **99ac** John Bauer, 'The Boy and the Troll or The Adventure', *Among Gnomes and Trolls*, volume 9, 1915; **99ar** Artepics/Alamy Stock Photo; **99bl** Granger/Shutterstock; **99bc** Universal History Archive/ Universal Images Group via Getty Images; **99br** Fine Art Images/Heritage Images via Getty Images; **101** Everett/ Shutterstock; **102** José Rico Cejudo, *Las Vestales*; **105** Library of Congress, Washington DC; **106–107** Hobbe Smith, *Floralia*, 1898; **108** The Metropolitan Museum of Art, New York, gift of A. I. Sherr, 1960; **109al** MB_Photo/Alamy Stock Photo; **109ac** Miguel A. Muñoz Pellicer/Alamy Stock Photo; **109ar** Zoonar GmbH/Alamy Stock Photo; **109bl** sanga park/Alamy Stock Photo; **109bc** Shikigami; **109br** Chris Willson/Alamy Stock Photo; **110** Heritage Art/Heritage Images via Getty Images; **111** Granger/Bridgeman Images; **112l** Fine Art Images/Heritage Images/Getty Images; **112r** C M Dixon/Print Collector/Getty Images; **113** Library of Congress, Washington DC; **114** Lanmas/Alamy Stock Photo; **115al** Peter Newark American Pictures/Bridgeman Images; **115ac** www.albion-prints.com; **115ar** Studio Canal/Shutterstock; **115bl** Universal History Archive/Universal Images Group via Getty Images; **115bc** Tim Graham/Alamy Stock Photo; **115br** Robert Harding/Alamy Stock Photo; **116al** Art Institute of Chicago, Chicago, Ada Turnbull Hertle Endowment; **116ac** The Metropolitan Museum of Art, New York, gift and bequest of Alice K. Bache, 1974, 1977 **116ar** PHAS/Universal Images Group via Getty Images; **116bl** Werner Forman/Universal Images Group/Getty Images; **116br** © The Trustees of the British Museum; **118a** The National Museum, Denmark; **118bl**, **118br** Mike Peel, www.mikepeel.net; **119a** © The Trustees of the British Museum; **119c** Adam Eastland/Alamy Stock Photo; **119bl**, **119br** © National Museum of Wales; **120**, **121** Andre Coelho/Getty Images; **122** The Metropolitan Museum of Art, New York, Rogers Fund, 1919; **123al** Peter Charlesworth/LightRocket via Getty Images; **123ac** Pontino/Alamy Stock Photo; **123ar** Rob Walls/Alamy Stock Photo; **123bl** Agencja Fotograficzna Caro/Alamy Stock Photo; **123bc** Black Star/Alamy Stock Photo; **123br** Jack Cox in Spain/Alamy Stock Photo; **125** Marc Zakian/Alamy Stock Photo; **126–127** Skyscan Photolibrary/Alamy Stock Photo; **128** Fine Art Images/Heritage Images/Getty Images; **131** © Christie's Images/Bridgeman Images; **132**, **133** The Cleveland Museum of Art, purchase from the J. H. Wade fund; **134al** Rob Walls/Alamy Stock Photo; **134ar** Pacific Imagica/Alamy Stock Photo; **134bl** Rob Walls/Alamy Stock Photo; **134br** Marcus Tylor/Alamy Stock Photo; **137** The Metropolitan Museum of Art, New York, gift of Ben Heller, 1972; **138** Icom Images/Alamy Stock Photo; **139al** © Sotheby's/Bridgeman Images; **139ac** Fine Art Images/Heritage Images/Getty Images; **139ar** Sepia Times/Universal Images Group via Getty Images; **139bl** Fine Art Images/Heritage Images/Getty Images; **139bc** FineArt/Alamy Stock Photo; **139br** Heritage Art/Heritage Images via Getty Images; **140** Wellcome Collection, London; **141** Pictorial Press Ltd/Alamy Stock Photo; **142** The Metropolitan Museum of Art, New York, purchase, Joseph Pulitzer bequest, 1917; **143** The Metropolitan Museum of Art, New York, gift of Henry Walters, 1917; **144l** De Morgan Collection; **144r** © Christie's Images/Bridgeman Images; **145** John Mahler/Toronto Star via Getty Images; **146** Christophe Coat/Alamy Stock Photo; **147al** Granger/Alamy Stock Photo; **147ac** The Print Collector/Alamy Stock Photo; **147ar** C M Dixon/Print Collector/Getty Images; **147bl** DeAgostini/Getty Images; **147bc** Leemage/Corbis via Getty Images; **147br** Luc Viatour/https://Lucnix.be; **149a** Moviestore/Shutterstock; **149b** Anna Biller Prods/Kobal/Shutterstock; **150**, **151** private collection; **152** Fine Art Images/Heritage Images/Getty Images; **155** Florilegius /Alamy Stock Photo; **156** Wellcome Collection, London; **157** Science Museum, London; **158** MeijiShowa/Alamy Stock Photo; **159al** bozmp/Shutterstock; **159ac** Dorling Kindersley Ltd/Alamy Stock Photo; **159ar** photo BabelStone, National Museum of China; **159bl** Leibniz Archive, Niedersächsische Landesbibliothek; **159bc** ART Collection/Alamy Stock Photo; **159br** I Ching Dice Pair; **160** SSPL/Getty Images; **161** Nik Wheeler/Corbis via Getty Images; **163** Active Museum/Active Art/Alamy Stock Photo **164–165** The J. Paul Getty Museum, Los Angeles; **166** © Christie's Images/Bridgeman; **167l**, **167c** © The Trustees of the British Museum; **167r** Wellcome Collection, London; **168–169** Bibliothèque nationale de France; **171** Design Pics Inc./Alamy Stock Photo; **172** © The Trustees of the British Museum; **173** Rursus; **175** Mikal Ludlow/Alamy Stock Photo; **176** Rafa Rivas/AFP via Getty Images; **179** © Hulton-Deutsch Collection/Corbis via Getty Images; **180** The Metropolitan Museum of Art, New York, Rogers Fund, 1914; **181al**, **181ac** Wellcome Collection, London; **181ar** PHAS/Universal Images Group via Getty Images; **181bl** The Cleveland Museum of Art, Andrew R. and Martha Holden Jennings fund; **181bc** Verbaska/Shutterstock; **181br** The Metropolitan Museum of Art, New York, gift of Florence Blumenthal, 1934; **182** Matt Cardy/Getty Images; **184–185** Adam Wiseman; **186** The Metropolitan Museum of Art, New York, Rogers Fund, 1931; **187l** Gianni Dagli Orti/Shutterstock;

**187r** PJR Travel/Alamy Stock Photo; **188** DEA/A. Dagli Orti/DeAgostini via Getty Images; **189al** Fine Art Images/Heritage Images via Getty Images; **189ac** Museo Nacional del Prado © Photo MNP/Scala, Florence; **189ar** The J. Paul Getty Museum, Los Angeles; **189bl** Fine Art Images/Heritage Images/Getty Images; **189bc** Artefact /Alamy Stock Photo; **189br** DeAgostini/Getty Images; **190** Hira Punjabi/Alamy Stock Photo; **191** Library of Congress, Washington DC; **192** Roberto Atzeni/123rf; **193al** Daniel Berehulak/Getty Images; **193ac** Oli Scarff/AFP via Getty Images; **193ar** Mike Kemp/In Pictures via Getty Images; **193bl** Jeff J. Mitchell/Getty Images; **193bc** Konstantin Zavrazhin/Getty Images **193br** Alehorn; **194a** David Tesinsky/Sipa/Shutterstock; **194b** Marco Secchi/Shutterstock; **196** Joan Gravell/Alamy Stock Photo; **197al** Detail of floor mosaic, Great Palace of Constantinople, Istanbul, Turkey; **197ac** Geography Photos/Universal Images Group via Getty Images; **197ar** © British Library Board. All Rights Reserved/Bridgeman Images; **197bl** Alex Wright/The Bellarmine Museum; **197bc** Art Media/Print Collector/Getty Images; **197br** Simon Garbutt; **198**, **199** Pablo Blazquez Dominguez/Getty Images; **201** © Homer Sykes/Corbis via Getty Images; **202**, **203** Hulton Archive/Getty Images; **207** Fine Art Images/Heritage Images/Getty Images; **208l** Bettmann/Getty Images; **208r** Library of Congress, Washington DC; **209** Dan Kitwood/Getty Images; **210** © Luca Tettoni/Bridgeman Images; **211al** Popperfoto via Getty Images; **211ac** Library of Congress, Washington DC; **211ar** Bettmann/Getty Images; **211bl** Christopher Pillitz/Getty Images; **211bc** Ed Jones/AFP via Getty Images; **211br** Joey Mcleister/Star Tribune via Getty Images; **212l** © The Trustees of the British Museum; **212r** The Walters Art Museum, acquired by Henry Walters, 1930; **213l** The Metropolitan Museum of Art, New York, gift of Mr and Mrs V. Everit Macy, 1923; **213r** The Metropolitan Museum of Art, New York, Rogers Fund, 1923; **214**, **215** © Pitt Rivers Museum, University of Oxford, 1985.52.2, 1985.52.275, 1985.52.1359, 1985.52.43, 1985.52.223, 1985.52.1370, 1985.52.957, 1985.52.705, 1985.52.254, 1985.52.1001; **216l** Universal History Archive/UIG/Shutterstock; **216r** Eileen Tweedy/Shutterstock; **217** Sean Sexton Collection/Bridgeman Images; **218** Library of Congress, Washington DC; **219al** Pep Roig/Alamy Stock Photo; **219ac**, **219ar** Witold Skrypczak/Alamy Stock Photo; **219bl** Mira/Alamy Stock Photo; **219bc** David Gowans/Alamy Stock Photo; **219br** Werner Forman/Universal Images Group/Getty Images; **220l** Design Pics Inc/Shutterstock; **220r** The J. Paul Getty Museum, Los Angeles; **221** Scott Olson/Getty Images; **222l** Peter Hermes Furian/123rf; **222c**, **222r** Serhii Borodin/123rf; **223al** 4LUCK/Shutterstock; **223ac** Mithrandir Mage; **223ar** AnonMoos; **223bl** TotemArt/Shutterstock; **223bc** Di; **223br** A. Parrot; **225** Alastair Pullen/Shutterstock; **226** Fine Art Images/Heritage Images/Getty Images; **229a** Kunstmuseum, Basel; **229b** Art Collection 3/Alamy Stock Photo; **230** Norman B. Leventhal Map Center; **231** *Langa Edda*, AM 738 4to f.43r/Cornischong; **232**, **233** Werner Forman/Universal Images Group/Getty Images; **234l** The Metropolitan Museum of Art, New York, The Charles and Valerie Diker Collection of Native American Art, gift of Charles and Valerie Diker, 2017 **234r** The Metropolitan Museum of Art, New York, The Charles and Valerie Diker Collection of Native American Art, gift of Charles and Valerie Diker, 2019 **235** Library of Congress, Washington DC; **236** V. V. Sapozhnikov, Photo Materials from Expeditions in the Southern Altai Region, 1895–99, World Digital Library **238** Sepia Times/Universal Images Group via Getty Images; **239al** DeAgostini/Getty Images; **239ac** Finnbarr Webster/Alamy Stock Photo; **239ar** The Metropolitan Museum of Art, New York, The Crosby Brown Collection of Musical Instruments, 1889; **239bl** ephotocorp/Alamy Stock Photo; **239bc** National Museum of the American Indian, Smithsonian Institution (19/8867), photo by Nmai Photo Services; **239br** © chrisstockphotography/Alamy Stock Photo; **240** © The Trustees of the British Museum; **241** Matteo Omied/Alamy Stock Photo; **242–243** The Metropolitan Museum of Art, New York, gift of Mrs Erna S. Blade, in memory of her uncle, Sigmund Herrmann, 1991; **244l** Science History Images/Alamy Stock Photo; **244r** Robert Harding/Alamy Stock Photo; **245** Library of Congress, Washington DC; **246** Fine Art Images/Heritage Images/Getty Images; **247al** Sheila Terry/Science Photo Library; **247ac** © The Trustees of the British Museum; **247ar** Forrest Anderson/Getty Images; **247bl** Science History Images/Alamy Stock Photo; **247bc** Sepia Times/Universal Images Group via Getty Images; **247br** The Metropolitan Museum of Art, New York, Rogers Fund, 1930; **249** Historica Graphica Collection/Heritage Images/Getty Images; **256** Eugene Adebari/Shutterstock

# INDEX

Illustrations are in **bold**.

## ACKNOWLEDGMENTS

I would like to thank everyone at Thames & Hudson who assisted in bringing this volume to fruition, especially Jane Laing, Florence Allard, Phoebe Lindsley, Georgina Kyriacou, Becky Gee and Tristan de Lancey. They have been a pleasure to work with. Thanks are due also to all who have encouraged my research and writing over the years. As always, special thanks must go to my family and friends for their support.

## ABOUT THE AUTHOR

Ethan Doyle White holds a PhD in Medieval History and Archaeology from University College London (UCL) and has a research interest in both European pre-Christian religions and modern Paganism. As well as having published over twenty articles in scholarly journals, he is the author of *Wicca: History, Belief, and Community in Modern Pagan Witchcraft* (2016) and co-editor of *Magic and Witchery in the Modern West* (2019).

**FRONT COVER**
John Collier, *Priestess of Delphi* (detail), 1891

**BACK COVER, SPINE & PAGES 6–7**
Nils Blommér, *The Fairies of the Meadow* (detail), 1850

**PAGE 1**
Green Man boss on the ceiling of the cloisters at Norwich Cathedral

**PAGE 2**
Francisco de Goya, *Witches' Sabbath*, 1798

**PAGE 4**
'The Raven Flood Totem', *Photographs of the Inhabitants of Metlakatla, British Columbia and Metlakatla, Alaska*, c. 1856–1936

**PAGES 8–9**
Chris Moorhouse, Druids celebrating the summer solstice at Stonehenge, 21st June 1978

**PAGE 256**
Eugene Adebari, Druid procession, 1980

First published in the United Kingdom in 2023 by Thames & Hudson Ltd, 181A High Holborn, London WC1V 7QX

First published in the United States of America in 2023 by Thames & Hudson Inc., 500 Fifth Avenue, New York, New York, 10110

*Pagans* © 2023 Thames & Hudson Ltd, London

Text © 2023 Ethan Doyle White

Designed by Anıl Aykan and Sara Ozvaldic at Barnbrook

Library of Congress Control Number: 2022945657

ISBN 978-0-500-02574-1

Printed and bound in China by C&C Offset Printing Co. Ltd

MIX
Paper | Supporting responsible forestry
FSC
www.fsc.org
FSC® C008047